BEING

ISN'T ENOUGH

The Truth About Eating

Meat and The Industry

Table of Contents

Preface 1

Introduction 4

Chapter 1: The Mistreatment of Animals in Society 8

Chapter 2: The Importance of An Animal's Life 20

Chapter 3: The Truth About Animals and Their Lives 33

Chapter 4: The Importance of Being Vegetarian/Vegan 47

Chapter 5: Meat is unethical and unnecessary 61

Chapter 6: The Dangers of Eating Meat 74

Chapter 7: Pigs Are Your Friend, Not Food 90

Chapter 8: Chickens And Cows Are Beautiful, Sociable Animals 98

Chapter 9: Treatment Of Animals Used For Food 106

Chapter 10: The Horrors of Factory Farming 112

Chapter 11: The Horrors Chickens and Fowl Face on Factory Farms 131

Chapter 12: The Torture Cows Face on Factory Farms 143

Chapter 13: The Truth About A Pig's Life In A Factory Farm 150

Chapter 14: Solutions To Factory Farming and Using Live Animals for Food 159

Preface

My passion for animals has led me to write this book. There are many who care about the plight of animals, but they have no idea what to do about it or they might end up going vegan or even becoming activists to help this situation and concern. There are also those who simply don't care about animals and never will. They eat meat and live their lives in happiness while the most helpless of creations live lives of suffering and become food for them. We are not at the top of the food chain.

We are simply barbaric people who feel we are living in an ethical and modern society yet resort to the most inhumane of practices towards the kindest caring and most compassionate creatures, the beautiful animals. They are the best creations and yet their short brutal lives are full of nothing but pain and torment? We need to change the practices that go on in this so-called modern and civilized society for if we don't do something about this it will never stop. We must fight for each and every animal and do what we can with our technology to save these innocents from the brutal and barbaric horrors of the farming industries as well as every area of life that causes harm to them.

Animal rights are an important part of our life and world. Animals are important beautiful creatures who exist in our world and it's our place and job to treat them with the utmost respect, love and care. Many times, people lack the desire to treat animals with respect and this is extremely wrong of them to do. Animals are just as important as you and I, and it's of utmost importance that we treat them with love, caring and kindness only.

Our world and planet is a great open space for every living being and creature and animals have just as many rights as humans should. Animals are beautiful, intelligent, caring wonderful creations of God who were placed on this planet for us to love and care for and it is our responsibility to care for them and give them unlimited love and respect, not consume them or treat them with disrespect. Being vegan and supporting the vegan movement is something we should strive to do, and the consumption of animals and factory farming contribute to global warming, climate and serious pollution issues in our world. Factory farming is an awful system and injustice to innocent farm animals who have no choice in the matter. Farm animals are subjected to heinous brutalities and horrible treatment and have to endure extreme amounts of pain and suffering, and the system needs to change, and new laws need to be implemented in order to protect these helpless creatures.

Introduction

It's important to understand the concept of fair treatment and respect and live in a world where the most innocent creations are given well treatment and extreme respect. We live in a society, in which we believe we're civil, yet are privy to committing heinous and atrocious acts against the best of creatures, and turn away from hearing upon the many grave injustices done to them and all the suffering billions must endure as a result of the lack of regulation of a very evil, callous, and cruel industry that doesn't care about their lives for a second, only profits.

Is being vegetarian enough to stop the evils that occur to these innocent lives who are destroyed day after day, repeatedly encountering extreme and harsh abuse and mistreatment, torture, and other atrocities? Does giving up meat help with getting rid of the evils that will always seem to occur as a result of an ill-regulated industry that doesn't care about the lives of billions and breeds billions of animals yearly only to be used as a steak, a chicken sandwich, or other forms of human consumption and food?

Being vegetarian surely is a must and necessity and works for sure to eliminate meat eating, however, the industry still remains and stands as there are billions of carnivorous humans who will elect to consume various forms of meats from every animal they can imagine, as if one or two doesn't sustain their hunger, greed, nutritious needs, or palates. Of course, humans can't resort to eating only a small portion or type of animal meat- the so-called 'civilized' human must resort to eating every creature including duck, hen, chicken, turkey, veal, cow, lamb, sheep, and the list is endless of course. That's because a civilized society would not be consuming these forms of animal meat, and if they did, would have created the most humane methods to breed these animals, and allow them a healthy decent life, and a very humane death, as opposed to the atrocities found in today's society and what has been occurring since factory farming has come into fruition.

Animals, the most important, precious, cutest and most innocent of creatures are not only abused, mistreated, and destroyed in heinous ways on this planet, but they are unfairly slaughtered in the most brutal of ways, without a voice, and without a care all because many out there are in dire need of a chicken sandwich. Or they feel that meat is the primary and best source of protein, that meat is a necessity in the consumption of human nutrition and diet, because there are few other options out there to eat, out of convenience, or just being born on this planet and in this society and brainwashed into believing that animal meat is one of the better substances to eat as opposed to healthy proteins that aren't a meat source, yet will provide even better nutrition than meat, and without the hazards and problems that animal meat presents.

This lack of regulation in the meat and dairy industry is a huge problem and epidemic in our society today and needs to stop and end. We are civil creatures and civil human beings with amazing and the greatest technology that we can imagine in our time and the most advanced form of it. Why is it that we are still consuming meat in 2024, a time when we thought in the 1980's, would be a highly advanced time full of more than technological gadgets but impossibilities such as the hoverboard as shown in movies, or greater technological innovations that have yet to come.

We are living in the best times in history, yet are still resorting to not only ignorantly consuming animal flesh as if it is nothing but the best commodity or means to sustain nutrition, but worse, we still haven't developed humane methods to allow these innocent animals whose lives are deemed worthless by the human race, who are bred by a careless industry only for food, and only to be mistreated worse than insects get treated by a mile, live in brutal, unsanitary horrifying conditions all of their life and face the worst fate and death of torture and other means of getting rid of their lives as if they never deserved a moment of peace or happiness?

Introduction

Who determined that the chicken or the pig were just random creatures that deserved to be bred by the billions and carelessly slaughtered as if they are nothing?

These animals will never wake up in the morning happy and cheery looking forward to their beautiful magical day like others who live in nature or with their families. They too deserve a life of happiness and to never have been born or bred into the horrifying reality they are a part of.

We mourn for the cat and dog, but what about the innocents who are destroyed daily and momentarily in the cruelest places to exist- factory farms. Every 16 minutes millions of innocent animals are cruelly and brutally barbarically slaughtered simply because we live in a confused careless society that fails to understand the way the industry works or simply just doesn't care enough about the needs and lives of innocent animals. The farming and agriculture industries don't care about these animals. All they care about are profits, but we should care. If we don't care about these animals, then no one will.

Chapter 1

THE MISTREATMENT OF ANIMALS IN SOCIETY

Animals Are Just As Important As You and I

Animal abuse is a worldwide phenomenon that is a huge problem in society today. The unfortunate reason for this is the ignorant belief many humans possess that animals are inferior to humans and that humans have some form of dominion over them. Animals are perceived in the world by the human species as being not as important, without a soul, and only there to serve the purposes of or to aid the human in doing what he/she needs. I've heard many people say this to me "well I like dogs because they'll do what you want." Humans perceive animals as being subordinates who are there for the human's desires, rather than being living, breathing, sentient beings who deserve to have a wonderful life of their own and to make their own choices, live their own lives, and who deserve to be treated with respect.

However, the truth is that animals are not subordinates, or inferior to humans, regardless of what any religious book or text seems to preach or teach humans. Humans do not have dominion over animals and should not have any place over any living creature period. Every life on this planet is important and matters. Every living breathing creature deserves an equal opportunity and chance at having a happy abundant and beautiful life regardless of its status in the food chain or the cycle of life. Animals just like humans, are beautiful creatures, born with a life, a soul, a purpose, needs, wants desires, compassion, caring, a personality, and intelligence. Animals deserve to live a happy life and deserve respect just as humans and every other creature on this planet does.

The mistreatment of animals is a huge epidemic that is plaguing our society today. We live in a highly civilized technological society yet can't seem to grasp the concept of ethical and humane treatment for innocent helpless animals who are also being bred solely to be food and for human consumption. Who says that Cynthia the cow deserves a life and fate of nothing but maltreatment and torture, only to end up on someone's dinner table because they enjoy 'eating steak.' We think we are civil creatures and people, but would a civil society ignorantly go through drive thrus constantly and eat the flesh of other animals as if it's no big deal or a necessity when in reality, there are hundreds of reasons not to eat an animal's flesh and body.

Animals are just like you and I. They desire happiness, love, joy and enjoy every minute of their lives. They live in a state of goodness and enjoy being alive and enjoying their life with their family and friends. Animals do have family, friends, nephews, nieces, are aunts, uncles and parents and each and every animal to exist on this planet deserves a life free of pain and suffering, and deserves to be in their natural environment and do not exist to be used or abused by confused, evil, selfish and very ignorant humans who do not care about the welfare of these animals or have flawed perceptions of them.

Between 17 and 20 million animals are used in research annually in the United States, most of those being rodents. At least 20 million dogs, 60 million cats, another 60 million feral cats, and an undetermined number of farm animals are exposed to painful procedures in the United States. Animals are often experimented on, brutalized, murdered, tortured, used for food and the list goes on. At least 20 percent of dogs in this country suffer from osteoarthritis. About 88 billion farm animals worldwide yearly are inhumanely bred, grown, and slaughtered for food consumption and not a single one endures a painless, humane experience of life or death, for there are absolutely zero painless and humane ways that humans have created to end an innocent farm animal or animal's life.

There are hundreds of brutal inhumane ways animals are treated on this planet. From factory farming to slaughterhouses, unjust, cruel animal experimentation, dog breeding and puppy mills, to animal confinement and death in animal shelters, and animals used for blood banks and money. Many greedy, evil, and sick humans use animals in a number of disgusting, sick, dirty and horrifying ways for profit or to assumably better humanity in some form according to them by using animal's bodies to experiment on or other sick, unfathomable, and unnecessary reasons. Animals are not on this planet for humans to use in any way, shape, or form, in fact the opposite is true. Animals are on this planet to live their lives just like we are, and if used to be companions to humans or to assist and help them in different arenas. Animals deserve nothing except exemplary worthiness and respect from humans, kindness, and nothing except good.

Farm animals and animals that humans consume were not put on this earth solely to be used as food for human beings. Cows, chickens, pigs, turkeys, and all animals are highly sociable beautiful creatures that all deserve a fair chance at life, the same way we do. They deserve to live happy, healthy fruitful peaceful lives full of joy, laughter, comfort, the same way we humans do. So why do we breed animals at high rates only to consume them and treat them as if they are produce or nothing except commodities, when they are living, breathing, sentient, souled creatures who deserve a chance at life?

No innocent animal deserves to be bred in the masses, the billions, and ignorantly and in the most evil and brutal ways, literally tortured and murdered in the most unspeakable heinous ways, with a horrifying life that even insects don't have to endure. It makes no sense to do this to living, breathing, sentient creatures with beautiful, gracious souls that possess the characteristics of love, goodness, and caring within them. Animals do not need to be bred in the masses and in the most inhumane ways in order for humanity to consume meat in any form, for humanity needs to cut down or eliminate the concept of consuming animal meat completely. Every living creation deserves a happy, healthy life and a chance at life, and if animals have to bred in the masses, there need to be new laws and regulations which regulate the manner in which these innocent helpless beautiful creatures are treated, and to ensure that they are allowed a good life that they deserve even if they are used for any form of slaughter or mistreatment.

With all the technology that we possess, we haven't come up with productive, ethical and efficient ways to efficiently put an innocent helpless animal to sleep or end its life in a humane way? Why are there no laws out there protecting these innocent animals that are used merely for a silly burger here and there, or because a human is in dire need of eating a burger, a chicken sandwich, or any kind of meat that can easily be substituted using vegetarian products, which make far more sense.

People often compare meat eating to what happens in nature. They claim that nature is about 'survival of the fittest', we are at the 'top of the food chain', and worse, that we are similar to animals who hunt their prey out of sheer necessity and no other options. All of these ignorant, arrogant notions are completely untrue.

The truth is that animals were not created to be food for humans or other creatures. Nature is very different. There are animals who use other animals for food yet do so under the pretense of a creature in nature searching for food and hunting it down or killing it. These animals are not grabbing animals in mass quantity and breeding and destroying them or skinning them alive or doing awful grotesque things to them. A lion may hunt down 56 deer in their life, while the human agriculture services dispose of billions of animals per year.

Animals are mistreated, abused, and hurt in a plethora of sad ways in society. From unjust and unfair animal experimentation to the household abuse of innocent animals from dogs to cats to all sorts of innocent creatures that exist, the list is endless. There is a vast amount of animal mistreatment that occurs in society everywhere and it is truly unfair and shouldn't ever be occurring.

Animals are living, breathing, sentient amazing creatures with great souls. Many are incredibly friendly, sociable and they have their own friends, family, and lives. Any living breathing creature that was born on this planet deserves the chance for a beautiful special wonderful life just like any human does. They were not born or created to be used abused tortured and then discarded and destroyed in a manner which is worse than how most insects are treated. This is unfair to these innocent creations and to their mothers, brothers, families, and to God.

Imagine being a piglet born in a factory farm. Piglets are warm fuzzy beautiful, adorable, cute little creatures that deserve to be treated with love respect and care.

Hansel was born on a factory farm. Imagine waking up every day to a small, cramped area where you can barely move, unable to be near your mother or family. Imagine knowing your fate just isn't something right. Imagine being in so much pain and then suffering only to know that you can't escape this reality and, worse, you are suddenly taken, and your genitalia is cut off. Piglets are not here on this earth to be used and consumed as pork or meat. They are cute innocent animals who deserve a living chance and good happy healthy lives. Every creature does.

Eating meat is not a necessity. We do not need to resort to eating large amounts of animal flesh in order to sustain our nutritional needs as human beings. Human beings are in fact, omnivores, and they eat a variety of substances. Humans do not need to eat or consume meat in order to sustain nutritious needs and especially in order to consume more protein.

Many people feel as if it is a necessity to consume the flesh of other animals in order to ingest specific vitamins, or in order to get the necessary amount of protein, however, this is far from the truth. The human body was not designed to be able to withstand the eating and consumption of meat and as a result, the consumption of animal flesh has, and will resort to a host and variety of health issues for the human being, whose body is not equipped to handle meat.

That juicy burger you're so thrilled to eat was once a living, breathing beautiful cow that lived a very tragic and harrowing, painful, gruesome life and was then brutally murdered simply because demand for meat will just never end it seems. There is a high demand for meat products, and it has increased since the 1960's. That cow deserves to be alive and healthy and living its best life just like many other animals get the opportunity to do so. It didn't deserve to be bred and raised for food, treated lower than anything to exist and then brutally slaughtered with no care for it, its family, mother or children.

Animals are living breathing creations just like you and me. In fact, they are exactly like us and there is no difference when it comes to feeling pain and having feelings emotions, having families lives, children, expressing their feelings, and having social lives as well. Animals are incredibly social creatures and have their own system and their own groups and gangs, and they are no different from human beings.

Growing up in south Florida we lived on five acres and had an extensive amount of land in our area. Our home was a large one, and since we had enough land, we decided to get a horse, two cows, and a family of goats and have our own mini farm. Cows are in fact just like any other animal, amazing, beautiful, gentle, loving, and kind creatures. They are extremely intelligent, beautiful, caring, cute animals and they make great pets and they're extremely friendly and nice creatures who are very sociable just like we are.

Some people claim well chickens are meant to be used for food. Since when? Why must such a highly technological society resort to such disturbing primitive measures just to sustain false nutritious needs or even to eat the flesh of innocent helpless creatures. Since when did chickens, cows, pigs, turkey, and ducks be selected to be used as creatures to be bred only for food while there are numerous alternatives to using animal meat as any form of food or for consumption.

True injustice is the harming of any helpless, living creation that cannot fend for itself, and this type of injustice is one that needs to be eliminated altogether specially when it comes to the notion of the inhumanity of how innocent animals are slaughtered, and treated and factory farms throughout the planet, and in every country and nation everywhere.

In a society or technology has prevailed, and we are at the latest and highest technological advancements in our current timeframe in state of world and error. We surely cannot come up with better ways, and methods of being able to humanely, steal the life of millions of animals in mass quantities rather than resorting to primitive disturbing methods which is what is what has been happening throughout history and society, especially in today's confused culture and world.

Those humans who feel as if innocent animal's lives don't matter, and as if they deserve to be bred solely for the consumption of humans are extremely confused ignorant people who have no idea what the concept of empathy, caring, kindness, or love is.

For if they knew what the concept of caring, kindness and love was, they would never for a second feel, as if innocent animals were meant to be bred and used solely for food rather than treating them with extreme respect, kindness, love and goodness, which is what they deserve and how they deserve to be treated only.

How can living, breathing creatures with hundreds of feelings be treated lower than any insect ever gets treated and as a result even have much shorter lifespans than any insect due to the monstrosities committed by the livestock and farming industry and those who support it by purchasing and consuming meat products?

We need to be more conscious and aware of what we're doing and not contribute to the evils the agricultural industry poses on animals and humans as well. We need to stop ignoring the severe animal crisis situation going on not only in the factory farming industry today and the global impact this has on the climate and the planet. We also need to do something about what is going on not only in this industry but the animal abuse situation that goes on everywhere from animal experiment labs to puppy breeders- animal abuse and suffering is a rampant problem in today's society and steps need to be taken to eliminate or eradicate these severe issues going on today.

Humans believe we are civilized creatures but really, we're not. Society may seem civil but that is just a guise behind all the abuse and evil that goes on secretly behind closed doors. The consumption of meat produced and slaughtered by the most brutal inhumane methods is part of this very inhumane uncivil concept that occurs in everyday life. People go to restaurants with their significant others, family or friends and order quail, duck, beef, steak and never care to think twice about the fact that the very thing they are consuming was once a breathing living creation that lived a very frightening painful tragic and unfair reality that it didn't deserve. People go to shop in their polos, dresses and have no realization of the lack of civility they possess for consuming these animals or contributing to the overall negligence or care of how these creatures are treated as animals being bred for factory farms.

You may go through a drive thru and order a chicken sandwich while living your human life in some semblance of peace or even extreme peace and happiness, while that burger you're eating had to live a life of deep pain and extreme tragedy. The lives of these innocent silent victims are ones that are in loathsome horrifying tragedy, and they are silent and cannot fight or speak for themselves their precious lives or their families and have been succumbed to a life of harrowing endless torture and one of the most brutal painful deaths that could exist. There are no true humane methods being used to breed, house, or slaughter these precious animals.

Simply being vegetarian, though it's a great choice to commit to and do and is a help to animals everywhere out there, just isn't enough to stop and end this vicious cycle of evil that goes on everyday today involving the lives of innocent helpless factory farm animals and animals everywhere. That is because there are still billions of carnivorous humans out there, who will ignorantly consume the flesh of innocent animals whose lives are something too horrifying to describe, and who are bred and born with no happiness, no hope in their life, and nothing except extreme torment, torture, suffering and pain that isn't even unspeakable, only for their tragic brutal lives to end with their precious bodies being used only as meat for hungry, confused human beings who never think twice about that chicken or turkey sandwich they so desire while rushing to Arby's hoping to have a 'quick lunch.' That quick lunch was a painful million-year torture session for that innocent animal whose flesh you're so ignorantly eating simply because people have been brainwashed into believing that 'turkey tastes good, meat is a necessity for b vitamins, and meat is necessary for protein'- all concepts that are completely false in nature.

Chapter 2

THE IMPORTANCE OF AN ANIMAL'S LIFE

Why do we as humans feel as if Johnny the chicken's life is less important than Johnny, the human's life when this is a completely untrue concept, and way of thinking. The chicken's life is just as important as Johnny the human's life and that is the reality of the situation.

A human's life is not more important than an animal's life and vice versa. Every creation is a living, sentient, breathing creature with intense extreme feelings, great intellect, thoughts, emotions, actions, and each, and every creation that exist on this planet deserves to be treated equally and with great respect, love, caring, and kindness, not with hatred, animosity, distain, objectivity, and many of the negative qualities that innocent animals are treated with.

Every animal and creation to exist deserves a fair chance at life, and a life free of any form of pain or suffering. To breed animals or take animals in and inflict extreme pain and suffering on them is something that should never occur for a second much less by the millions daily, and billions yearly. An animal's life is extremely important, and they have great feelings just like humans do and deserve a fair chance at a peaceful happy life, so does every living creation to exist. Our own class, Mammalia is being bred and tortured at alarming rates all while being construed as 'legal' and 'humane' by standard practices and laws and there are no legality issues with the brutal manner in which these innocent animals are being treated momentarily and there are no laws to protect their welfare.

Animals are not lesser or inferior creatures like many humans ignorantly feel or believe they are most of the time. Animals are living sociable creatures just like us who have emotions, thoughts and feelings, and thinking exactly like we do most animals, in fact, possess even more than we do as human beings, and they actually possess intuitive capabilities that humans do not have access to.

Those who do evil are amongst the confused for doing evil, is not a normal thing to undertake or do. It is not normal for human being to want to do evil, or to another or to harm another.

It might be what humans will tend to do, but it is not normal or natural to commit an evil or crime against another person, creation or thing. Committing an evil is a grave sin against humanity and a grave sin in general. We want to stray away from committing any evil actions or deeds and head towards the path of goodness and beauty and loving positivity. Evil is not that which we hold ourselves accountable for it is in fact, that which human beings will do or tend to do and turn around and pin their misdeeds onto another person.

Those who commit crimes against others will learn the hard ways through the laws of nature and of the world and the atrocities that come with doing evil or misdeeds against another. Those who commit these evils against another, are already the lost, the strayed the confused, and those who are the bane of society. They already lack the wonderful qualities that make up a good human being in a good person and it is their loss for choosing to be the kind of person that they are.

Each and every animal's life is of extreme and grave importance. There is absolutely no such belief or concept that the lives of animals are inferior to those of human's lives, for this makes no rational sense to a civilized or ethical nation or to anyone who thinks in a rational manner. Every animal that is created on this planet has immense feelings, a social life, a family, and deserves to live a life of beauty and comfort just as we humans do. The mass breeding of innocent farm animals for the use of food needs to end anyway, and if not there need to be major alternatives for the manner in which these animals live and die, which needs to be changed into something completely humane. After all, with all the technology that these monsters possess, they are still resorting to the most brutal of treatment of these animals which is completely unnecessary and is beyond unethical and should never have existed in the first place in a society in this day and age that deems itself 'civilized.'

The silent victims of unspeakable brutality

Imagine being a mother cow and having your baby being stripped away from you suddenly knowing he isn't going to face a good fate. The cows are in horror while this is happening and know something awful is going on and how wrong this is. Unspeakable brutality happens to animals not just in factory farms, but on the planet everywhere. There are animal experiment labs, dog breeders, and people who abuse animals in their own backyards. Animals need our help to help end and eliminate as much animal abuse as we're able to do. They tend to be at the end of any form of brutality and evil and it's unfair to these precious souls.

Animals possess a conscience and understanding

Animals possess the notion of conscience and know when something isn't right or when they are being abused or mistreated. Animals are not stupid creations that lack awareness of these things. On the contrary- there are many humans committing these evil unjust acts who have no care or knowledge of their extremely evil behaviors. The animals involved know that something is gravely wrong, and that what is happening is not normal or ok and they have no voice to speak out.

Animals know when they are being abused or mistreated. They lash out or harbor feelings internally. These factory farm animals will often resort to crying out or asking for help though most of them know their situation is hopeless. They are in the clutches of an industry that has no regulations and just doesn't care.

Animal's lives aren't just important, they are just as important as a human's life or moreso. Animals are living, breathing, sentient creations just like us and every animal deserves to live a happy and healthy life just as we humans are able to live most of the time.

The Farming Industry isn't regulated

Why can't the farming Industry just have regulations or care? What would happen if they did? Why can't they treat any of these animals with the respect and humanity that they or any living being deserves- will it hurt anyone?

We're living in the 2000s- an era of supposed technological advancements and yet, there is no regulation of how animals are treated in these factory farms and worse, there are no real alternatives to animal meat that are being implemented in mass population around the globe or world.

Humans don't need to eat meat to survive. Humans were really not even meant to eat meat. Meat contributes to a whole host of physical and mental conditions that humans are incapable of being able to deal with.

Animals are helpless voiceless creatures

Animals are innocent helpless silent creatures and victims. They have no way of speaking out and no way of defending themselves. As humans we are living peaceful happy decent lives while these innocent animals are living in death houses just on the line to be brutally destroyed. They don't deserve this reality and fate. They at least deserve at the very least decent living conditions and a humane death, something that these wealthy factory farm owners can give them yet refuse to. They could care less because there is no one regulating this sickness. There is no one there to stop these people from committing the evils abuses and atrocities they do towards these innocent animals.

Animals are a gift to us

Animals are full of love and light. They are full of blessings and peace. Animals are like children and even more innocent. They do not possess rage, hostility, hatred, vengeance or evil. They are only good and carry with them love, joy, and kindness. They, unlike humans, are full of goodness, love and caring and are not there to betray, hurt others or do evil lascivious acts. Animals are a gift bestowed to us and we can allow them to live the happy comfortable lives they deserve or take them in as companions and children and allow them to bless our lives with their beautiful presence.

We have the choice to help out these innocent silent victims.

We have the power to stop this heinous evil and these awful atrocities that go on in these tragic circumstances and to help these innocent animals whose lives and bodies are treated as if they are nothing and really treated worse than inanimate objects or even insects. Why are these animals treated in such a brutal and horrific manner even when being killed rather than being slaughtered in somewhat of a humane way? Their lives matter and their feelings matter greatly. Every creature is of utmost importance and these animals are no less than we humans are.

We have to be advocates for these animals.

We have to be the advocates for these animals in these factory farms. For if we're not, no one will ever stop or change what is occurring and this industry will never be regulated. The industry has no regulation, and nothing is ever done about the inhumane evils being done to these animals. Sitting around and being vegetarian or vegan is a great start to helping animals, but there will always be millions and billions of meat-eating careless people out there who have no care or concern for these innocent animals.

We need to be proactive and do something about this situation and be advocates for these animals and give them rights too, rather than ignoring the situation and not doing much for them. Being vegetarian is one wonderful way of saving animals, but the planet isn't going to turn vegetarian. We need to educate others to become vegetarian and more importantly, take proactive steps to help organizations get the laws changed when it comes to animal rights and the many abuses that occur towards these helpless creatures. Even once laws get changed, nothing really happens. We need to figure out ways to get measures put into place that emphasizes that these laws become enforced in some manner. They need to be enforced in some way because they just aren't and as a result billions of innocent animals are being brutally murdered because humanity and factory farming have gotten out of hand and just don't care about anything except eating meat or profits.

Animals need a voice

Animals everywhere need a voice. They have none sadly. They are the most special beautiful and amazing beings and yet humans feel they are above them in some form. However it's just not true- humans are definitely not above any animal.

Every animals life is precious. Their lives are just as important as ours and sometimes even more so due to all the beautiful, wonderful qualities an animal possesses.

Animal Rights

An animal possesses, the same rights that a human does, and each and every animal to exist, deserves to be treated with nothing but respect, kindness, beauty, love and light, and with no form of ill, malignant, negative, or harmful treatment of any form or nature. Animals are beautiful, intelligent, amazing creations of God, and they, in fact possess great, intuitive capabilities, and wonderful capabilities in general by which they behave and act, and they expect the same treatment in return but more than often don't always receive it.

It is extremely important to give animals the rights and respect they deserve. They are not puppets or objects who deserve to be abused, mistreated, and destroyed as if they have no feelings. Animals have the exact same feelings we do and, in some cases, even stronger ones, and they do not have a tolerance for pain as some people might ignorantly believe or feel. Animals are more delicate than humans and have far less of a tolerance for pain and in many cases, zero tolerance for any of it. They feel pain, grief, and sadness just like humans do and, in some cases, even more so. Animals are extremely intuitive creatures and may even have psychic abilities and have extreme senses of perception and some even possess the capabilities of extra sensory perception. Animals need to have these other abilities in order to survive and to enhance their regular abilities and senses.

Animals need thousands of humans advocating for them, being their friends and helper and helping them out, not joining the conglomerates of companies out there and destroying them or using them for food. Humans are of above average intelligence and are on this planet surviving and thriving and living their lives as best as they can. They have a choice most of the time on how they seek to live to be, why can't animals have this same choice in their own life? 72 billion animal's lives are destroyed every year and used for food. This number is beyond staggering and extremely unfair to these innocent souls raised strictly for food on these horrifying factory farms that are simply just horror places for these innocent beautiful souls.

Animals are not created to be meat and food. An innocent chicken has to be raised in horrific devastating disturbing conditions and then put on a horrifying conveyor belt of death that is unnecessary and beyond inhumane and is usually heated to death in order for a human to consume a simple chicken sandwich.

People go through drive thrus every second of the day, shop at the supermarket, and go out to eat at high end restaurants in comfort, joy, and luxury and never think twice about what they're consuming. In order for a person to consume that simple so-called "delicious" chicken sandwich you may not even think twice about, take for granted or care for, some innocent chicken and his family had to suffer in a destructive horrific factory farm for weeks before it was finally mistreated in the worst way possible and skinned alive and had its throat cut and then it was boiled to death while still being alive a lot of the time.

Humans don't even think twice about the burger they're consuming or the piece of steak or where it really came from. They just "love steak" "can't live without it" or feel they need it in some form. They don't worry or care about the animal they are consuming or the amount of suffering it had to go through as a sentient living caring thinking intelligent creation having to come to grips with the reality that their life isn't a happy normal one and that they were living in a horror land full of pain torment injustice evil and suffering only. These animals didn't have an ounce of happiness or hope. Was that fair to them? Just for someone to drive through and grab what seems to be a harmless tasty burger, an innocent cow had to live an unfair life of hell or torment or unjust brutal pain, and a senseless brutal death. It makes no sense to a rational thinking intelligent creature that any of this had to even happen.

Where are the people who will stand up for or help that cow out- was there anyone to help him or her out? Of course- there was no one. His life wasn't less important than someone's next door neighbors' life. He was a living intelligent sentient creation. He had feelings of love, joy, happiness, and desire. He felt pain just like any other creature and longed for peace and goodness. His life was extremely important. He wasn't just a "cow" bred for food simply because he was born on a farm that is there to make sure he was only raised and then inhumanely unjustly slaughtered.

Every living food you eat was an extremely important breathing life and creation just like yourself that deserved a good life just like you did. Every animal was a healthy functioning thinking creation of God that never deserved that life or fate even for a second. They are silent voices unable to fend for themselves, with no one to turn to or complain to, and no one who would help or vouch for the pain and torment they had to endure something that they called life as a creature bred only for food.

Being vegetarian doesn't mean eating nuts or vegetables all day or having a lack of protein. There are thousands of foods you can eat, and vegetarian cooking is actually extremely delicious. Chicken inside a rice dish isn't really that necessary nor does it make the rice dish taste any better. You can easily substitute most dishes you eat, prepare, buy or make with vegetables and they will taste almost exactly the same.

It doesn't mean you must eat tofu all the time or only as your primary source of protein. Humans are not lacking in protein and there are many alternative sources of protein such as anything except for meat. Every food contains some protein, and you can substitute some humane seafood choices with mammalian choice meats. Animal meat is also an unnecessary part of any kind of food that is to be consumed. It makes no sense to me why people even cook goat- for the meat is tough, hard to eat, and not good for the human diet.

Chapter 3

THE TRUTH ABOUT ANIMALS AND THEIR LIVES

Animals are highly misunderstood creatures in this society and always have been since the beginning of time. Many humans have come to false terms when it comes to animals and feel as if animals are inferior to humans in some form and just not as important, when this is completely untrue.

There are many myths and misconceptions when it comes to understanding animals and their lives. They are just like us humans- they have lives, their own families, a social life, friends, food, and have to hunt and live their life just like a similar cycle of life just like any other living being on this planet. Why are animals so misunderstood and why do people feel as if animals' lives just don't matter as much?

A lack of understanding, miseducation, ill education, ignorance, and many other factors play a part in why people seem to be so misinformed when it comes to animals. A family member of mine once said "well cats are selfish creatures, they only care about themselves, and only come to you when they want food or water." I can't even imagine the many number of times I've heard people say that false statement about the precious, amazing, and precocious cool cat species, which is the complete opposite of that ignorant belief that people seem to hold about them.

Animals are loving, caring, kind creatures and they definitely are our friend and were not meant to be food for us. A family member who is part of a religious group told me recently that animals were put on this planet to be food for humans. I said really? You believe pigs were meant to be food for humans? Well, what about the lion, tiger, and zebra? This just doesn't apply to them right only those unfortunate pigs, dogs, cows, chickens, goat and sheep, lamb, ducks, and turkeys who are bred and cruelly harvested for their meat when we as a planet can easily come up with healthier meat substitutes and use those rather than having "the real thing" as most ignorant humans feel about the subject.

Animals desire a good life too. They want to wake up to a great reality and future, peace and joy. They get excited and have a passion for living life more often than humans do. Animals become extremely happy and feel grateful and blessed when they are in a good situation and know it. They know when they are in a good home as well and are well taken care of and possess nothing except happiness and are in the knowing that they are safe and comfortable.

The intelligence of animals

There is also a common misconception that animals aren't intelligent creations or aren't as intelligent as humans, though this is highly untrue. Animals in fact are just as intelligent as humans and in many cases even moreso! They actually possess other abilities, and intuitive capabilities and have other senses which far surpass that which humans do have. While humans have their five senses the sense of smell, taste, touch, sight and sound, the senses of animals are far heightened, and they have abilities that far supercede what a human does possess.

Animals are extremely intelligent creations and do not carry intellect that is inferior to that of humans. They in fact hold the same or a similar level of intellect as humans and many may even be smarter than their human counterparts. Humans may possess the ability to write, but animals, just like humans talk and communicate the same way they do, form close bonds and relationships, have friends and lovers, and give birth to children and harness families.

Many animals such as pigs, chickens, and cows have demonstrated a similar intellect to each other and share a similar intelligence with many primates. Chickens have shown they can solve puzzles, while pigs sing to their babies while young. Mammals are in the same class as humans and do harbor the same intellectual skills that a human does.

Animals possess intuitive abilities

Animals do have the characteristics of extreme intuition and can sense certain concepts and things unbeknownst or not understood to most people. I once went through a harrowing and terrible experience and wasn't home for a few days. Once I got back, my cat just stared at me with the notion of "I'm so sorry this happened to you" and wouldn't leave my side. Now, this is a common thing you may hear from others- that they were gone for a period of time and their pet or child (pet) responded to their lack of presence, yet there is something far deeper that is going on when it comes to an animal other than the fact that someone was gone and the animal simply just missed them and reacted to this.

There is a lot more that goes on when it comes to an animal's response to their parent or 'owner' being gone for an extended period of time, and the truth is that is an intuitive one. Many animals possess the characteristics of great intuition, a sixth sense, and can sense and know specific things that are happening. Talk to anyone who is taking care of or who has a cat or dog or other animal living with them. They can corroborate with the notion that many animals seem to have a sixth sense about things and situations.

Humans usually rely on their five senses, yet animals do have additional abilities and sensors that enable them to detect changes in their environment. These senses often allow them to foresee events, respond to danger and even connect with people on a deeper level.

One aspect concerning animal intuition is their amazing ability to detect natural disasters before they occur or right before they happen. Many animal owners have reported strange activity and behavior in their pets, moments before an earthquake or a catastrophic event. Animals are believed to be able to detect changes in the Earth's vibrations, electromagnetic field, and in the atmosphere which allows them to potentially foresee these scenarios that are occurring.

Animals have the unique ability to pick up on danger or dangerous events or situations, and have an innate ability to understand a human being's emotions. They can read body language and understand a human's mood or emotions or circumstances that are going on with regards to a person. Pets can sense emotional cues and provide support and comfort to someone. Many pet owners have even claimed to experience telepathic communication with their pets.

Animals are sensitive to energy and can pick up on different energies and moods. Animals simply possess this concept in order to protect themselves in natural environments, and they do have heightened abilities in general. This allows them to detect when there is a potential threat nearby. They seem to have an internal radar that helps guide them towards safety or warns them of danger.

An animal is not inferior to a human

Animals are not inferior to humans and their lives are just as important and significant as a human's life.

Why do we as humans feel as if our lives are more important than an animal's life and why do so many ignorant humans feel as if they are more worthy than an animal. Just the notion of calling an animal an 'animal' is simply wrong and untrue. These creations we call 'animals' aren't just simply 'animals'- they are extremely important, beautiful creations that are just as important as humans and their life is just as important as a human's.

Many people just don't feel this way. They feel as if an animal's life is less important than that of a human's or that animals are inferior to humans and don't deserve the kind of life a human does. They feel humans are entitled to having more than these animals and this is simply far from the truth.

Animals are highly misunderstood

Animals are a very misunderstood species. There are many different areas in which people in general hold and harbor many false and unfair notions with regards to animal's lives, how they live, and how they truly feel. People have come to a huge misunderstanding that animals either don't have feelings, don't feel pain, or aren't sociable, social creatures with their own bodies and lives who deserve a good life the same way humans feel other humans do.

The complete opposite is true- most animals, birds, and mammals are highly sensitive, have great feelings and often even have greater feelings than human beings. They, just like humans, and any living being are extremely sensitive to pain and feel pain just like any person does. There have been numerous faulty untrue studies done that make erroneous claims that animals feel less pain or aren't responsive to or don't feel pain at all. Yes! Of course, animals feel pain, and many are more sensitive to pain than human beings. Animals just like humans do have pain receptors just like us and feel pain immensely and in some cases their tolerance for pain is far less than a human's tolerance but is definitely equivalent to a human's tolerance for pain.

Animals feel just like we do

Animals are highly sensitive, beautiful intelligent creations who feel, think, experience and live just like we do. They feel all kinds of emotions and aren't just ignorant creatures who have no idea of anything. They possess and experience a range of emotions. Animals feel pain and suffering. They have feelings just like we do. They feel jealousy, pain, remorse, guilt, anger, frustration, fear, confusion, and can distinguish different feelings within themselves and in others. They harbor a plethora of emotions and not only behave like little children which many people feel, but they act just like regular adults do as well.

Animals feel and experience trauma and can manifest symptoms of PTSD and react and respond to a variety of experiences and painful experiences in a similar manner to humans. Their emotions, reactions and range of emotions are very similar to that of a human's. Animals are not emotionless creatures who have no response, memory, or fear of things. They just like a human possess a wide variety of feelings, emotions, and responses. Cats and dogs fight amongst each other, friends, siblings, and there are territorial and responses of jealousy that are evident and boldly present within the reactions of animals.

There is misinformation going around from faulty studies that animals do not feel pain the same way humans do but this is just a false concept and idea there to misinform people and further create more issues for the already serious animal crisis situation that is taking place in society and in the world today. There is a plethora of misinformation from 'cats are selfish and don't care about anyone or anything,' to 'dogs lack intelligence', to animals don't feel pain and are numb to it.

Mammals share the same nervous system, neurochemicals, perceptions and emotions all of which are integrated into the experience of pain, claims Marc Bekoff an evolutionary biologist and author. Animals have the same pain receptors, and their nervous systems have the same structure as humans. Scientists have developed specific 'scales' which are indicators of pain and what an animal is feeling, and each animal has their own unique characteristics which they display when experiencing pain.

Animals usually cry out or respond when they are inflicted with any form of pain, and this is one of the few responses or stimuli and proof that animals do feel all kinds of different pain emotions. Animals do harbor greater smell receptors and taste receptors so it's very possible they may actually harbor a greater number of pain receptors that people do. Animals, just like humans, not only feel physical pain but feel a range of emotional pain and do mourn the loss of friends and family and those close to them in a similar way that humans do.

Reptiles, amphibians, and fish have the neuroanatomy necessary to perceive pain, according to studies. Reptiles avoid painful stimuli and pain-killing drugs reduce this response- these are both indicators that they experience pain.

In the wild, species such as rabbits will avoid showing pain, so they don't get singled out as an easy target for predators. Hurt rabbits will stiffen their whiskers, narrow their eyes and pin back their ears. Predators in the wild such as wolves behave in a similar manner and will mask their pain in order to not appear vulnerable to those around them.

Animals are deep thinkers and possess a conscience

Animals are not ignorant, shallow, confused creations that hold no semblance of intellect, morality, rationale, or the concept of right vs wrong. Everytime an innocent calf is born and snatched away from its mother, it knows exactly what is going on. It knows this isn't right. It knows it belongs to its mother, and vice versa. The calf bellows out in despair so does the mother, as if "this isn't right, someone stop this." They call out in despair for someone to help them, but there is no one around in this cruel and careless disgusting industry that will ever help these innocent voiceless precious souls. The manner in which they just snatch the cow away from its mother and take it away forever makes no sense, even for profits. There are numerous ways companies can gain profit while allowing innocent calves to live, and by not mass breeding cows in major quantities.

Animals know the difference between right and wrong. They know what evil is and that hurting someone just isn't good or right and shouldn't be done. You can perceive this notion from any animal you have come into contact with but more so with those who have been mistreated or abused.

Animals not only know and understand these concepts, but they are in fact very deep thinkers. From turkeys to pigs, animals are thinking, responsive, rationale very intelligent creatures who know exactly what is going on in their own lives, and often in the lives of their human owners or parents.

Animals are extremely good creatures

Most animals except for natural predators that hunt other creatures or humans are generally extremely good and decent beings. Cats and dogs are not evil by nature, and most animals hold or carry the sense of goodness in them. Of course, there are some animals that can hurt or harm others or humans, but that's a different story. Animals carry with them the concept of love and goodness and most of them enjoy being good, happy, peaceful, pleasantly sociable creatures and live in harmony with their human parents/owners or with each other.

Most animals out there are not out to hurt others unless it's something that has been ingrained in them due to environmental circumstances or reasons. Animals just like humans enjoy living good, happy, and natural lives and make friends with those around them whether it be humans or those of their own species or a different one.

Animals deserve to be treated only with respect and kindness

Animals are extremely peaceful, loving, kind, very caring creatures who give out enormous amounts of love and good and they enjoy getting this in return. Most animals are very peaceful good creatures and deserve nothing but the best treatment from humans especially. Sometimes they may not be able to get it from other animals though it's usually not a problem, but humans have the conscious choice to treat these beautiful kind souls with nothing but goodness, a caring attitude, and love.

Animals love to be treated with kindness, and they will give it in return tenfold and much more. This goes for all kinds of animals from cats, dogs, to goats, sheep, cows, pigs, chickens, and all those farm animals who people don't think twice about as pets or who people don't seem to care for as much.

Animals rarely take for granted the fact that someone is feeding or taking care of them. They possess a higher awareness and understand that they are very lucky blessed creatures, even if it's something that has been going on for a long time or is something they are used to. Animals have a deeper understanding of life and concepts and far more than we give them credit for. They simply don't sit around feeling entitled to getting the food and care that is given to them by their human owners/parents.

Animals are not pets

Animals who humans take care of are rarely or can hardly be thought of as pets. Really there is no such thing as a pet. When someone takes an animal to care for in their home, the animal is literally a part of their family. An animal isn't a cute little 'inferior' or lesser 'pet,' that many people tend to label or perceive this creature as. This beautiful creation can be thought of as more like a roommate or cohabitant, or a child of theirs because that is usually what is going on. A human parent or owner is providing for this animal and giving them food, water, and shelter and allowing them into their home and is introducing them into their place as a part of the family.

We need to do away with labeling and misunderstanding the concept of animals as lesser or inferior creatures that are 'pets,' or those who we own, when the reality is they are not really pets and we don't own them- they are simply a part of our family and become roommates or our children in a sense. Animal's bodies belong to them. They have children, friends, siblings, parents and they have their own lives. Their lives belong to them and not to us. They are worthy of and deserving of living a happy and fruitful life, each and every single animal to ever exist on this planet and nothing else.

The life of an animal is extremely important. Their lives are just as important as ours, or even more due to them being so vulnerable. They were not put on this planet or created to be used as food or to be bred and treated lower than millions of insects put together or to be bred solely for food or used to experiment on. Every animal to exist has feelings, a life to live, their own thoughts, emotions, beliefs, and are deserving of the kind of lives humans are allowed to live.

Animals have their own lives, and their bodies belong to them and to God. No animal on this planet is allowed to be used, abused, or mistreated in any way, shape, or form by any human being or other creature for that is not the way nature was intended to be. No human has the right to touch or harm another animal or feel as if they have the right to do this for their own sick reasons for every animal has the right to live a happy, peaceful, and good life and that is the reality of the situation.

Chapter 4

THE IMPORTANCE OF BEING VEGETARIAN/VEGAN

A civilized and ethical society would never resort to eating meat, I mean we should know better, shouldn't we? With all the technology we possess, and the tools we have as humans- our minds, developed brains, ability to think, cook, prepare all kinds of foods, and our ability to communicate with one another with such refinement, precision, and advancement, we should use all our utilities to do something good for the planet and for the animals and should have ended this meat-eating barrage and horror centuries ago, not made it worse.

But of course, humans have done the opposite. Rather than advancing mentally and technologically for the greater good of others and of animals, humans have resorted to the most barbaric, primitive and disgusting, disturbing brutal methods of eating meat by terrorizing and torturing animals to their death, brutal deaths, and global and mass destruction of billions of animals worldwide all in the name of protein, meat and food.

Being vegetarian or vegan is a very important part of being a highly conscious, caring, decent human being on this planet, and is a very important part of living in this society to protect the 88 billion animals that get bred for food and slaughtered worldwide just to satisfy the palates and digestive systems of misinformed and ill-educated people who seem to not know any better.

Vegetarians don't eat any form of animal meat such as cows, pigs, goats, chickens, fish etc. Vegans don't do the same, but they also do not consume eggs, dairy, milk, cheese, or any other product derived from an animal. It is important to be vegetarian, but more important to be vegan as well. The reason for this has to do with how cruel the dairy industry is when it comes to how it treats these innocent cows and chickens only for profit and to keep the hunger of humanity for these products satisfied. We as humans do not have a necessity to consume eggs, dairy products or any products that come from cows because it is not natural for us to eat these products. They also were not meant for us to eat them.

Humanity can be construed as a selfish animal milking creation that treats animals as if they are a commodity to be used, abused, tortured, and murdered unjustly just so we can eat the products of these creatures, when we can create similar products from other sources and do not need to consume any of these products from the mass destruction and slaughter of innocent helpless beautiful animals.

Vegetarianism seems to be a misunderstood concept in this society. People feel as if vegetarians have their own set of beliefs, apart from the norm, are a part of their own society and some people almost feel as if it's their own religion. This is far from the truth. Vegetarianism is a conscious and humane choice to not participate in consuming the flesh of helpless innocent animals on this planet, and to consume other healthier choices such as vegetables, fruits, legumes, and the hundreds of many other options that are present for humans to consume.

It is important to understand what constitutes being a vegetarian and why it is so important to follow and practice this lifestyle of abstaining from and foregoing any form of animal meat. Many vegetarians and vegans have a passion for animal rights and are against the farming industries out there and the evils and unjust abuses that many innocent animals have to endure. As a result of witnessing this pointless evil, many people unable to stop this have turned to abstaining from meat and all animal products completely as a way of protesting the evils, a method to try to stop or eliminate it altogether, and as a way of stopping the concept of eating meat and doing away with any and all animal abuses that are occurring as a result. A vegan does save almost 200 animals every year, but that is not enough. Billions of innocent animals are destroyed every year enough to make it to the moon and back 42 times around. What that means for the planet is global destruction and extreme waste that is produced from the hazards of the manner in which these animals are treated and discarded. They are treated lower than waste products and as if they are only dispensable commodities and not living breathing sentient creations.

It is important for our health and the planet to become vegetarian but more importantly to become vegan and forego and eliminate all animal products from your diet, and to never support the corrupt, cruel dairy or any part of the farming industry. Being vegetarian is wonderful, but becoming vegan is even better for the corruption and evils that occur towards chickens, hens, and dairy cows as a result of this industry is too awful to describe, and it's important to live a life of abstaining from all animal products because we as humans were never meant to consume animal products and have no need for them.

A plant-based diet is the healthiest diet to have for the human body is not designed to properly digest meats which can lead to a host of health issues. The benefits of a vegan diet are outstanding and comparable to a meat diet this is something that every person needs to focus on doing and becoming- completely vegan. People feel as if being vegan seems difficult and that there aren't many options for food in this scenario, but this is further from the truth. There are thousands of different types of food that can be created and consumed using a healthy and delicious plant-based diet and a wide variety of different types of foods that can be created that are both healthy and good tasting.

Veganism Protects Your Health

Benefits of a Vegan Diet

There are numerous myths and false ideas that surround the concept of a fully vegan diet. There are false beliefs that a vegan diet lacks protein, calcium, iron, b vitamins and other nutrients essential to health but this is not the case. On the contrary, you can get every essential nutrient needed from a vegan diet and a plant-based diet is shown to not only protect a person's health from various diseases and ailments such as cancer, heart disease, stroke and diabetes but it also provides antioxidants that are essential for healing the body as well.

Plant-based sources such as tofu, spinach, almonds, lentils and mushrooms can provide all the nutrients a human needs to sustain nutritious needs. The vegan diet is not deficient in any major nutrients and can actually create a healthy manner of living and eating as opposed to eating animal meat. Plant based and vegan diets are rich in fiber, vitamins, minerals, and antioxidants that help protect against diseases. Plant based diets also tend to be lower in unhealthy saturated fat and cholesterol.

Studies have shown that plant-based foods lowered the risk of type 2 diabetes by 23%. They also found that men who ate a vegan diet had a 35 percent lower risk of prostate cancer than those who incorporated animal foods in their diet. People who follow plant-based diets also have a lower risk of cardiovascular diseases and can better maintain their weights and cholesterol levels.

Reduced risk of cancer

Research shows that the best diet for cancer prevention is a plant-based diet. Many people tend to argue that white meat is completely safe for humans to ingest, but the truth is humans were not designed to digest meat properly and the best diet for humans is a plant-based diet.

Meat contains carcinogenic compounds that promote cancer development. On the other hand, plants have antioxidants and produce chemicals that protect cells from various forms of damage. Plant foods are linked to a reduction in cancers that are common in meat-based societies.

Reduced risk of stroke, diabetes, and heart disease

Studies do show that people who consume meat have a high risk of developing diabetes and heart disease. Researchers found that consuming red and processed meat increased a person's risk of heart diseases by 15 percent and diabetes by 30 percent. Research shows that plant-based diets lower the risk of cardiovascular diseases and heart attack.

Improved immune system

A healthy immune system fights off the risk of infections and helps protects us from other diseases such as cancer. Plants contain vitamins, antioxidants, and minerals that actually strengthen our immune system and fight off microorganisms.

Phytochemicals and antioxidants that boost our immune systems also neutralize toxins from pollution, viruses, bacteria and preservatives from processed foods.

Better digestive health

A plant-based diet can improve health drastically and stop disease in the body by feeding good bacteria in our digestive tracts. People who consume a vegan diet have the healthiest gut flora which tends to help against conditions like heart disease and diabetes.

Veganism saves the planet and environment

On top of the horrifying evils that are done to animals, the concept of eating animal meat has tremendous disturbing harmful effects on the planet as well. Animals being used for meat are in need of sustainable nutrition and these animals are producing extreme amounts of waste which cause co2 emissions in enormous amounts. Plant based meats and legumes have a lower climate impact than animal meat.

Livestock require land and water as opposed to legumes or nuts. Vegan meals are typically the most environmentally friendly and should be the option that people use when it comes to consumption. By switching to a plant-based diet, a person can reduce carbon emissions by 7-10 times less than by eating chicken or beef.

According to research, addressing the dietary needs of a future global population of ten billion people necessitates a huge reduction in animal product consumption by adopting a planetary healthy diet. This is primarily a planet-based diet. This would actually result in a 13% reduction in greenhouse gas emissions compared to the staggering scenario that is going on right now.

14.5 percent of all human-caused greenhouse gas emissions can be attributed to livestock farming. This industry produces carbon dioxide, methane, and nitrous oxide, which all contribute to global warming. All factory and animals farms are a source of greenhouse gases. Cattle, sheep, and goats produce large amounts of methane.

Most greenhouse gas emissions from plant-based foods are far lower than those linked to animal-based food. The farming of livestock and animals has a very damaging impact to the environment causing not only global warming but extreme direct pollution everywhere.

The global livestock industry also uses supplies of freshwater, destroys forests and grasslands, and causes soil erosion. The pollution of fertilizer and animal waste create dead zones in coastal areas and smother coral reefs. Livestock accounts for 50 percent of antibiotic use and there are also concerns of antibiotic resistance. The land used to rear the animals needs to be taken into consideration, the land, water, and fertilizer used to grow the grain to feed the pig and the pollution that results as well.

Most solutions suggest a plant-based diet to end global warming and all the pollution that is associated with livestock farming.

The Dangers Of Livestock Farming

It causes forest fires and deforestation

Industrial meat is the biggest cause of deforestation around the planet. In countries such as Brazil, farmers intentionally set forest fires clear space for cattle ranching and to grow animal feed for farms in the UK.

It causes climate change

The impact on the climate that meat has is very severe. This is actually equivalent to all the vehicles and airplane emissions in the world. Meat production accounts for 57 percent of greenhouse gas emissions of the food production industry. When forests are destroyed to produce meat or livestock are raised on farms, tons of carbon dioxide emissions are released into the atmosphere which makes global warming far worse. The trees are left to rot away on the forest floors which further creates worse issues for the climate.

Healthy trees are essential for absorbing CO_2 from the atmosphere. Without healthy trees, we are being thwarted in the fight against climate change for the positive.

Food is responsible for up to one-third of global greenhouse emissions with meat being the main source of the problem. It also represents 80% of deforestation and 70% of freshwater use. Livestock animals emit carbon dioxide, and the livestock production creates extreme pollution conditions of emitting carbon dioxide and methane two very harmful and noxious gases on the planet.

It's responsible for killing wildlife

The industrial meat industry in fact clears forests, destroys animal living spaces and habitats, and uses pesticides to grow animal food. For this reason, it is contributing to the extinction of thousands of animal species. Most of the land that is cleared for animal agriculture was home to a plethora of different plant and animal species. When these plants are destroyed and the animals have nowhere to go, this causes a loss of biodiversity and 60 percent of biodiversity loss is related to the meat industry.

Biodiversity is the variety of life in our natural world and can be measured by the number of different species that share a certain region. Biodiversity is a good indicator of the health of an ecosystem. A thriving a good biodiversity is a necessity for healthy ecosystems, which create a secure food supply, clean water, and essential medicines. Keeping biodiversity systems intact actually keep humans healthy.

Biodiversity loss can be described as the loss of life on Earth ranging from reductions in genetic diversity to the collapse of entire ecosystems. It has become a huge epidemic in society today and is only growing worse. Some scientists feel we are in the sixth mass extinction of animals going on.

Biodiversity loss is a critical scenario that is happening due to the industrial meat industry, factory farming and the lack of regulation that is going on. While biodiversity is crucial to a habitable planet and climate change in a positive way, the loss of biodiversity and pollution issues that are occurring as a result of the global meat market has become a huge epidemic in society today and as a result is destroying the climate as we know it.

It pollutes the air we breathe and water we consume

Factory farms pollute the air we breathe due to the excrement produced by the animals. Every second our nation's factory farms create 89,000 pounds of waste that contain dangerous concentrated chemical and bacterial toxins without waste systems incorporated.

This waste is often just dumped into lagoons, or it is erroneously sprayed on fields causing bacteria and chemicals to poison our air and water every single day. Many people become sick as a result of this hazardous waste.

Toxic gases and bacteria from excrement become a part of the air we breathe and get distributed over a wide area simply by the wind. Factory farms will spray liquid manure into the air, and it gets dispersed by the wind to other surrounding areas. It is a disgusting method they use when the holding areas of urine and fecal matter are full.

People who live near factory farms harbor the threat that their water systems will be very contaminated by the waste and excrement of animals. Their water systems are in fact highly contaminated from the waste of factory farm and farm animals.

As a result of this toxic pollution and contamination, people can suffer health problems from asthma and brain damage to birth defects, memory loss, and even respiratory problems along with many other issues due to air and water contamination. The threat to people's health as well as the climate is a huge problem the livestock and agriculture industries are creating for animals as well as people out there.

It releases greenhouse gases causing global warming

Meat production contributes to the release of greenhouse gases including carbon dioxide, methane, and nitrous oxide. The accumulation of these gases in the atmosphere leads to severe global warming. Raising farm animals in such massive numbers is one of the major reasons to these greenhouse gas emissions. These ruminant animals in fact digest their food in such a manner that releases methane and nitrous oxide. The corrupt damaged industry is also responsible for the release of these greenhouse gases through transportation of animals, the slaughter process, and through feed production.

Veganism saves animal and human lives

Billions of innocent animals are brutally slaughtered in factory farms, farms, and throughout the planet everywhere. Being vegan helps to end the horrific massacres that are happening everywhere with regards to these animals, and it not only saves animal lives, but human lives too. Humans are very affected by not only the climate changes, but the mass pollution that occurs as a result of the agriculture and farming industry, and a host of health issues can occur as a result of these dangerous and faulty factory farms that exist and the many faulty methods and practices they use.

Veganism needs to become the norm for everyone

Veganism is a beautiful and gracious movement to sustain human nutrition through plant-based needs and it is the most important concept that people need to understand needs to be practiced. Veganism needs to become the norm for the planet. It is often misunderstood that veganism creates a deficiency in vitamins or proteins for a human's body, but this is just a myth and far from the truth. The many vegetables that do exist along with legumes, nuts, seeds, and other components that make up a vegan diet actually can provide the proper sustenance and nutrition for human beings.

Veganism not only saves factory farm animal lives, but it saves human lives, a vast number of other animals affected by the climate issues the meat industry creates on this planet and helps the planet significantly. It is important to not only become vegan and vegetarian and focus on the living this kind of lifestyle with the way we eat and think, but also to educate others when it comes to living this way, being, thinking, and existing. It's important to be vegan, stay vegan and teach others the importance of being vegan in order to save animal, human lives and to help the ecosystem of the planet.

Chapter 5

MEAT IS UNETHICAL AND UNNECESSARY

Meat consumption has increased in recent decades with it doubling since the early 1960's according to the Food and Agriculture Organization of the United States. Studies also show that wealthier nations consume more meat. The meat consumption per capita for industrialized nations is staggering compared to those of the developing world. Over 88 billion land animals are raised and slaughtered for food production every year. This is unfair to the billions of innocent animals being bred solely for food in a society where technology seems to be prevalent and during an era where something can be done about the ignorance that is occurring in this situation.

Livestock farming occupies more than a third of the world's habitable land area. It can actually take between 5,000 and 20,000 liters of water to produce a kilogram of meat. Producing one kilogram of beef actually requires 25 kg of grain and 15,000 liters of water. The impact meat has on the global environment is staggering and is only getting worse as time goes by.

It is falsely believed that meat provides valuable nutrition for most humans, but the opposite is true. Meat does not provide any real nutritional value and the nutrients you can find in meats such as iron, zinc, b vitamins, and protein you can find in plenty of other vegetarian sources as well. Meat contains no fiber and is a dangerous cholesterol elevator and worse, is linked to many and various health related issues in humans. The human body was not designed to eat meat.

Humans are omnivorous creatures and do not need to consume meat in order to stay healthy, in order to thrive and survive and in order to sustain their nutritious needs. Meat simply does not hold any real nutritious value for human beings and does more damage than it does sustain human nutrition. It is in fact linked to numerous health issues and studies have linked meat to an increased risk in diabetes, heart disease, cholesterol levels, inflammation, cancer and a list of many health disorders present in humans.

Meat is not a necessity

The consumption of meat is not a necessity for humans of today, where other sources of food are readily available. Whereas humans feel animals are there for their consumption and taking as they want, the reality is that meat-eating is unnecessary, unethical, cruel, and every animal deserves an equal chance to live and a good life, just as humans feel they deserve a chance at life.

Meat eating has been done since the beginning of humanity when there were available sources of meat for humans to hunt and consume. The cave people of the past and other hunters and warriors depended on meat and other forms of animal life for survival and in fact behaved similar to many predators out there in nature today who rely solely on this source for food and survival. It's understandable that in the past, homo sapiens, homo erectus, and many species of humans had no other sources of food, so they had to hunt for their meals. However, is the consumption of meat a necessity in today's day and age, where we as humans who are omnivorous and live in a society where all kinds of foods are reality available to us, have wide varieties of all kinds of foods at our disposal, as well as the luxury of 'meat?'

I believe it is not in any case. We as humans in today's so-called 'civilized' society have every kind of food imaginable to us from grains, to snack bars, to crackers chips, nuts, seeds, tofu, soy, soups, breads, and all kinds of engineered creations being thrown our way every year created from various sources. Sure, the average human enjoys beef, steak, chicken, fish, seafood, and all kinds of meats, but is the concept of consuming meat absolutely necessary for our survival, and worse, the mass murdering of billions of innocent animals who are produced solely to be used as human food, bred and not given a chance at any form of life, enjoyment or pleasure? Not only is it not necessary, but it is an absolute abomination to mass produce innocent animals for the sole purpose of them becoming food for humans, not giving them a chance at life, pleasure, or enjoyment. It is cruelty and a deviousness that is welcomed and accepted because of the human belief that these animals' lives are of no importance and are allowed to be only created and used for food purposes.

A cow is being bred, to produce calves, those of whom are going to live their very short lives, in tiny crates and boxes where they will never see sunshine, or daylight, where they can barely move or turn around, and will be fed concoctions of varying liquids in order to produce a more tender distinct form of veal for the human consumer. Animals are being bred and used only for food sources, with no care for their lives, their worth, their desires. Is this a humane thing to do? It's one thing to be a hunter/gatherer from the past and have no food sources and have to shoot down your prey in order to eat, but to live in a world where animals such as chickens, cows, pigs are being bred on mass levels, tortured, used, abused and then slaughtered cruelly is a completely different concept. This is not only murder, torture, its cruelty and it should

NOT be happening in a civilized society where we have the option of eating MANY other forms of food out there.

Are you really going to tell me, that people are stupid enough to compare human farm factories where millions of animals are brutally tortured starved and slaughtered cruelly to simba the lion who NECESSARILY has to kill or hunt down some prey in order to live and survive through the very circle of life, and cycles of nature? It is of course NOT the same thing nor will it ever be. Simba the lion is not mass torturing large numbers of animals in order to consume its meal. The lion, tiger and other animals are just doing what they have to do to survive and eat, and this is ok. It might be horrific for the innocent animals who are killed, but this is nature, and how nature works. The lion doesn't have the ability to go grab some nuts off a tree, eat a fruit, or buy a bag of chips. The lion must eat what's available to him. Nature is NOT the same thing as the human mass torture of millions and billions of animals at a catastrophic and disgusting horrendous rate in order to appease the palates of millions of spoiled and selfish human beings who have no care for the lives of any of these innocent animals.

Some may interpret that religious books speak of animals being there for the humans to enjoy, consume. Even in those past days, there was no mass torture of animals. There were farms, and animals were given adequate land to live on then slaughtered in a humane way. So if God was speaking to humanity through those books, he was letting those prophets know that animals can be consumed by humans, if so, yet the animal is surely NOT meant to be bred, created in mass quantities in factory farms just so they can live a short hideous cruel and brutal life, only to be tortured and murdered by cruel humans who treat them as if they are nothing.

However, many of these religious books in fact speak of the beauty of animals and that they are there to benefit and help humans in many forms, yet rarely even talk about animals being there to be used as food solely. Animals are there to help us in many ways and can be of benefit to humans through a multitude of resources. Animals help humans healthwise, and companion animals can be of great help to those humans with disabilities and health issues.

These animals' lives matter, EVERY animal's life matters and has meaning and worth. Chickens do not deserve to be bred to be used, nor do cows, pigs or any animal on this planet. You'd think that in a civilized society we would know better. In THIS modern civilized society, we would have done away with animal consumption all together!! With all modern technology out there, we can't create a product that is similar to meat, tastes like meat, so we can in fact eliminate the consumption of animal meat altogether. Are you telling me that in a society so highly technologized that we can't come up with products SIMILAR to meat that taste even BETTER than meat, to resort to over mass murdering millions of innocent creatures??

Not only do humans not NEED to eat meat, they do NOT need to create large farms to mass breed and torture and cruelly treat these innocent beautiful animals who DESERVE a CHANCE AT LIFE and whose lives should NEVER be created solely for the purpose of being consumed or being consumption for human beings. Every animal's life matters- each and every animal is a LIVING, BREATHING, sentient creature with feelings, emotions, love, respect, who DESERVES a chance to live a happy life. No animal is created only to be used for food. Animals are loving, caring beautiful creatures who deserve the same chance at life that every human does. They are intelligent beings who are fully aware of everything that is happening around them. Humans lack the awareness or compassion for these innocent creatures who have no voice and no say in what happens to them. While it is not always the fault of the human who lacks awareness and isn't forced to really care about the conditions in which these animals have to endure and suffer, humans have a right and duty to do what they can to protect and help these millions and billions of innocent animals who suffer mercilessly just so humans can have their flesh to eat. All while this is completely unnecessary since humans are omnivores and capable of eating anything and have plenty of other food sources and options at their disposal.

Animals are living sentient creatures who deserve respect, love, care and in today's 'modern' society we need to find a way to come up with alternatives to meat and remove the concept of meat-eating altogether and protect the future of the species of this planet and stop the madness that has been ensuing with the cruel and unethical treatment of farm animals, and animals being used for food, and find a new solution and alternative for this civilized planet.

Human Psychology- To Dominate Everyone Else

Unfortunately, we live in a world where humans feel they are at the top of the food chain, this bizarre 'evolutionary desire' to sustain themselves and their species and to display this dominance by having power over all the so-called 'lesser creatures' on the planet and within this food chain. Darwin calls it 'survival of the fittest' and though it may exist, in a so-called civilized culture and society where we as humans have the ability to use our most moral and noble aspects over our primitive and animalistic ones, we should be focusing less on survival of the fittest and more on the equality of all species and living in harmony and balance with our fellow creatures on this planet. Humans with all their supposed superior mental abilities, capabilities and strengths, ability to rationalize, analyze, have moral discern, the ability to distinguish between right and wrong and even go deeper into analysis of life, spirituality, ethics, should be the top of the food chain species, who use their powers for good, not evil.

Humans need to be the big brother to stand up and do good and be the righteous moral high road takers. They need to protect the other species and do only good on this planet- use their mental capabilities to help their own species and to be a moral role model to all living beings, and promote integrity, strength through love peace and harmony, do good and protect all the animals out there. This is why humans are given these abilities and strengths- to use them for good, and to aid embed protect love nurture cherish help. Instead, humans take all the wonderful superior qualities and strengths given to them and what do they use them for- that's right, to bully, abuse, denigrate, destroy, slaughter, terrorize and destroy other creatures and species and to bully and dominate them using some kind of lower animalistic behaviors which civilized and moral humans of our time should be past.

So, humans take their wonderful qualities and characteristics and use them only to do more harm and bad, rather than to promote growth, equality, and harmony- shame on them. With this immaturity, lack of morale, lack of humility, and utter chaotic state of mind, many humans rather than treating animals with the respect and dignity they deserve, turn to using their pathetic positions as 'humans' to abuse denigrate and have dominion over these innocent creatures, who on the other hand, possess none other than the beautiful traits of compassion love kindness caring and giving. These so-called 'animals' who are deemed so 'INFERIOR' by humans, are the ones yet possessing and exhibiting all the positive and superior traits and qualities which humans despite all their supposed SUPERIOR mechanisms and functions given to them by nature, have NO CONCEPT of displaying showing or possessing. How ironic this is- and yet humans believe themselves to be the superior creature? I beg to differ..

Possessing a 'unique and capable' mind does not make the human biologically superior to any other creature. Throw a human in a cage with a lion and you will find out who wins and who loses. Each creature and species have their own set of characteristics and qualities, which make them who they are. The cat is not superior to the dog, and the dog is not superior to the goat. Each and every living creature and species is made up of the qualities which make them who they are. The human in fact is the INFERIOR being, who being given so much power and place in this world, has used their power and status only to do cruel acts, evils and seek to hurt or bring others down, destroy the planet, torture other creatures and themselves and act like the sickest of creatures out there period. Humans, by common logic are far from superior in many ways- they are inferior in many ways.

Meat is extremely unhealthy

Meat is completely unnecessary for humans to consume. Humans are equipped in the most generous of ways with a very large capacity of choices of food, varieties of food, types, flavors, brands, names, and yet humans still have an irrational and unnatural need to resort to eating animals and meat thinking it is a grave necessity for proteins, vitamins, or they simply feel that without meat, they would have nothing to eat! This is completely untrue in the harshest of ways

Why must humans add more animals to their list of murder and unfair slaughter such as goats, lamb, ostrich, and any other animal they feel it's fair to consume simply because they are humans and animals aren't human. Humans might ignorantly say to one another- have you tried gator! Frog legs?! Snail? They rarely think of the implications or the concern associated with the statements they're making regarding the consumption of these innocent creations, and the pain and torment these animals have to go through as a result of being on the menu worldwide for ignorant, confused, selfish, and greedy humans.

Do humans need to eat this many different kinds of animal?

Duck? Quail? Turkey? Chicken?

Why on earth do humans feel a need to just murder and kill this many different animals for food- especially when meat is not needed or necessary? Humans don't even need to eat animals at all to live, survive, be happy or even have their bellies full or for any form of sustenance! Animal meat is extremely hazardous to a human being's body anyway. Being vegetarian or vegan doesn't mean that humans have to eat nuts all day and lack protein. Animal meat is a very unsafe way for a human to even ingest or obtain any form of protein.

So why do humans have this unfulfilled desire to consume even more fowl and various animals? Humans surely don't need to add duck, ostrich, and other living fowl to their menu simply because duck might taste good in some form or just because they might find it interesting or fascinating or even delicious.

Consuming different forms of bird or various animals is not interesting or even remotely intelligent and makes no real sense. Various fowl are not meant to be food for confused greedy selfish humans who have beyond an abundance of food choices, and just have more of a selfish desire to add more animals to it because in their minds, an animals body really doesn't matter or because they've become conditioned into thinking this way.

Humans do not need to consume various kinds of fowl and only add to being even larger murderers of helpless animals when in reality, one type of fowl is enough to sustain them for a lifetime. However, it is unjust to even consume one type of animal for it is unfair to those particular animals who have to live a life of sorrow and torture only to be discarded, used and tortured so they can be food on a human's plate. This is unfair to any of the animals who are being bred solely for food in the livestock and agriculture industry, which possesses an extreme amount of injustice towards the innocent, helpless animals that are born into it.

The manner in which these higher thinking and amazingly intelligent mammals and fowl are tortured and abused is too horrifying to describe. How many different forms of animals do humans feel they need to consume or eat, and whose precious lives need to be stolen unjustly.

Animals have feelings just like any other creature does. They have lives and families. They are social beings and have duties in their lives, are parts of social groups, create clans and gangs, have children and love and care for their children, fight with each other, feel bonds with their siblings and parents just like humans do. Animals are not objects that can just be used as humans please for money, sport, food or for other sick purposes simply because they can't fend for themselves or have no one to help them or can't speak up about these atrocities.

Being vegetarian simply isn't enough, nor is being aware of a certain issue. Helping others gain awareness of this issue also isn't something that will aid the plight of the current situation that these innocent farm animals must face. It's extremely important to stop eating all forms of meat, and to educate the masses about the importance of vegetarianism and veganism, and to attempt to end meat-eating altogether on this planet, but it's even more important to figure out ways to get the laws changed and to get any laws that are in place to be enforced in order to protect the voiceless, beautiful innocent creations whose lives are something too tragic to begin to describe.

We feel any kind of evil or cruelty done to any human is gravely wrong yet ignore what is done to any animal. Everyone turns the other way and ignores what these animals have to endure the kind of unfair lives they are forced to live. People just think "oh that's terrible or sad," yet rarely think- is there something I can do to change this situation or to help these animals or is there something that can stop these atrocities that are taking place. This isn't just a simple solution it's one where a lot of laws and practices will have to be changed and practices that a lot of twisted people just don't want to stop for some reason.

Chapter 6

The Dangers of Eating Meat

The Dangers Of Eating Meat

Meat dominates the planet. From fast food restaurants, to the finest of dining, the primary feature on every menu seems to be 'meat' very sadly. There seem to be few other options or alternatives out there. The sad reality is that humanity and humans have become extremely conditioned and ingrained by society into believing that there are few options out there and even the fact that meat is not only a necessity but a monopoly out there when it comes to food substances that are readily available for consumption.

When you go to McDonalds- you don't find salads on the menu anymore, or any healthy vegetarian or vegan options. They have monopolized their menu to hamburgers only or fried chicken sandwiches. Menus are so dominated with meat, many people feel as if there are very few options out there. Humans have become so brainwashed into thinking that animal meat is the norm and that there is nothing wrong with its consumption. They mock vegetarianism and even feel if people eating only 'turkey' on their sandwich are 'missing out' on major ingredients and elements.

Very few people, maybe only the small percentage that make up vegans or vegetarians might think about the food that people consume and the hazardous conditions that meat produces on the planet, along with the health implications of consuming meat, and the dangers the billions of animals bred for food face on a momentary basis. People rarely feel guilty or saddened by the thought of eating any form of meat. They are usually elated and have become so brainwashed into believing that the meat of animals is meant to be food for humanity.

People have become brainwashed into eating meat

People are so confused and feel that there are no other options. When they open a menu all they see is 'ahi tuna,' to 'chicken sandwich.' Burgers, chicken, shrimp, tuna, and every kind of meat you can imagine graces the menus of human diners, kitchens and restaurants and the idea of where these meats came from seems to bother very few people. Though places are becoming more vegan friendly with the 'impossible' brand being on many burger menus these days and the 'chick-un' brand growing as well, menus with great vegan friendly options are a large stepping stone away from this reality.

People claim they want to 'eat the real thing', which makes little sense. Who would want to 'eat a real living being' or a 'real chicken' as opposed to a 'fake chicken' made out of healthy vegetables that might even taste like real chicken. Consuming real flesh and blood makes little sense to anyone. The desire to consume flesh and blood is disgusting and not natural to humans anyway. Who in their right mind would readily crave a real animal's true flesh and blood and wouldn't want a substitute knowing that they are not murdering and consuming living, breathing creations that deserve to be alive and happy living their best lives the same way we are.

I would never want to eat the 'real chicken,' only the fake thing which would be a wonderful substitute and not even the substitute. I would prefer a healthy vegetable or grain like quinoa or couscous over any form of meat whether real or fake because it makes no logical sense to think that a dangerous carcinogenic substance that is harmful to my body is something that I would crave all the time or even want to consume.

Meat is not a necessity for good human health

Animal meat is not only not a necessity for essentially good human health, on the contrary it is the biggest contributor to a myriad of severe health issues that humans face. Meat eating has been associated with 25 different health issues, including type 2 diabetes, cardiovascular disease, and bowel cancer. The environmental impacts of meat production and its contribution to climate change also make meat a threat to human health.

Meat does the opposite of giving good health to a human- it creates extreme forms of disease, raises cholesterol levels, instills food poisoning, and causes a host of various health problems in a human. While meat may contain some essential vitamins that are known to human health, the negatives outweigh any benefits one might get from consuming any form of meat.

Human bodies are not designed to digest or intake meat

Humans may consider themselves to be omnivores, but the truth is humans haven't always eaten meat throughout the history of time. The concept of agriculture started only 10,000 years ago when it became more convenient to herd animals. Research has shown that humans lack the basic abilities to be effective or good hunters and not well equipped biologically or physically to be hunters of prey or were ever meant to be predators the same way most carnivores are.

Humans possess specific capabilities and can easily be gatherers and have the ability to cook foods, and all types of substances that exist on this planet that were more meant to be consumed by the human species rather than the dangerous animal meats which only do harm to the body. There is no benefit from eating any form of animal meat, whether it be protein or any type of vitamins. This is all a myth, spread in order to brainwash the masses.

Humans have soft fingernails and very small, dull canine teeth. All true carnivores have sharp claws and large canine teeth that are there to tear flesh without the help of any kind of equipment. Humans have flat molars which carnivores lack, allowing us to grind up fruits and vegetables with our back teeth like herbivores do.

The human's teeth are in fact similar to those you would find in herbivores. Our teeth are large and lean on one another. The incisors are flat and are there to be used to peel, snip and bite soft materials. We do not possess the teeth carnivores do or chew the manner in which they do in order to be able to navigate meat and flesh.

The make-up of human saliva also proves that humans were not meant to eat meat and that our bodies are designed to ingest plants primarily. Human saliva contains the enzyme, salivary amylase which is responsible for the majority of starch digestion. The human digestive system has a narrow esophagus and can only handle small soft balls of thoroughly chewed food.

Humans and herbivores have small mouth openings and jaw joints above the teeth. This makes the jaws much weaker and less effective for capturing and killing prey but does provide the right mobility needed to crush and grind plants and other substances.

Carnivores and omnivores have sharp, pointed short teeth for tearing flesh. They have long and sharp canines for capturing, killing and tearing prey and flesh. Herbivores and humans have flat, long, front-teeth for cutting plants.

The human digestive system struggles to handle meat due to the length of the intestinal tract. All carnivores have very short intestinal tracts and single-chambered stomachs so that meat can easily be digested. Carnivores possess a digestive system that is capable of being able to handle a large amount of meat that can easily be digested in one sitting.

True carnivores are able to eat large chunks of raw flesh, and they have strong stomach acids that are able to break it down and kill any serious bacteria that would normally sicken or kill a creature.

Herbivores, on the other hand, have long intestinal tracts which are designed to breakdown various forms of plant foods and fibers effectively and absorb their nutrients as well. Humans have intestines that are 10-11 times a person's body length.

Humans have much weaker stomach acids- those that are similar to animals who digest fruits and vegetables. Dining on animal flesh can give an herbivore food poisoning. Every year in the US alone, food poisoning kills more than 3,000 people and sickens more than 48 million.

Studies have concluded that human beings have the gastrointestinal tract of an herbivore. After comparing the gastrointestinal tract of humans to that of carnivores, herbivores and omnivores, the conclusions have been made that the humans GI tract is created solely for a plant-based diet.

A physiological look at humans reveal that we are best suited to consuming a plant-based whole food diet. Our jaw structure, intestines, teeth, the chemicals in our stomach, all prove this to be the situation. The human body is in fact meant to function on plant-based foods that contain fiber, antioxidants, essential fats, and healthy low amounts of protein.

Meat is not a necessity for protein intake

People are often concerned about not getting enough protein, however, in industrialized countries where meat and dairy products are heavily common and easily accessible, more often than not people are eating far too much protein, and this can have serious health repercussions. Most Americans consume more than double the amount of daily recommended protein. High levels of protein intake have been linked to cancer, obesity, heart disease, and various kidney diseases and problems.

Meat is not a necessity for protein intake, unbeknownst to most people who feel that meat is a necessity for protein sustenance or

B vitamins when it is not. Humans are omnivores meaning they can eat a variety of foods and are not by nature carnivores, so it's not necessary that we as humans eat any form of meat.

People often ignorantly feel as if meat is a necessity for any form of protein when in reality, it isn't at all. The American research association has done extensive studies on the idea of meat eating and each and every conclusion has come to the same result- meat is definitely not a necessity for giving a human being the protein necessary for good or better health or to even maintain health.

The human being is an omnivore, and with a food supply of so many ready-made foods, snacks, a world of a variety of thousands of foods out there, the human is hardly in a situation where they would be lacking protein of all substances, for the substance protein can be found in almost every food you can imagine.

Humans are not lacking in protein and are in dire need of protein in order to thrive and survive. Humans are able to get the essential amount of protein they need to live and be healthy simply by eating a plant-based diet. The human body is not designed to ingest meat and it becomes an acidic creation in the human body. Humans have been brainwashed into believing that extra protein is a necessity for good human health, when in reality humans generally consume beyond adequate amounts of protein, are often in danger of consuming too much protein, and have bodies that are not in dire need of large amounts of protein specifically from animal meats which are in fact a hazard to the human body.

Red meat is hazardous for your health

It doesn't seem like news anymore, but eating animal flesh is bad for you. Very bad. But as well as increasing the risk of certain types of cancer, a study out this week has found that eating red meat and poultry is also linked with higher occurrences of nine common non-cancerous diseases including heart disease, pneumonia and diabetes.

Red meat contains nitrates which are harmfully derived substances that can lead to an increase in dangers for the health such as cancers or certain mutagenic compounds. There are claims that meat contains many important key nutrients, but you can get these nutrients from far healthier substances that can even affect a person's health in a positive way, rather than consuming fiberless meat, which is known to do severe health damage to the human body.

Meat has been shown to increase levels of oxidation. Amines that are produced when meat is heated at high temperatures are known to cause DNA damage as well

The World Health Organization already classifies unprocessed red animal flesh as a group 2A carcinogen, and processed meats like sausages and bacon in Group 1 together with smoking cigarettes, but until now their link to the leading non-cancerous causes of hospitalization has not been studied.

Using data from 475,000 middle-aged adults gathered over four years of the 25 most common non-cancer diseases regular intake - that being three or more times per week - of "unprocessed red meat, processed meat, and poultry meat consumption was associated with higher risks of many severe health conditions."

These include ischemic heart disease, pneumonia, diverticular disease, colon polyps and diabetes in relation to processed and unprocessed red meat; while higher poultry meat intake was associated with higher risks of gastroesophageal reflux disease, gastritis and duodenitis, diverticular disease, gallbladder disease, and diabetes.

The human body was not equipped or designed to break down or digest meat properly and it becomes trapped in the body for long periods of time. Meat and milk products are known to be acidic and create pus and acid in the body and are known to be very toxic to the body.

Poultry is dangerous for the health

What is the purpose in eating this kind of substance when all it does is damage to a person's health? People often argue that chicken, turkeys, and other fowl were made to be used for human consumption, yet this is just not the case and can't be further from the truth. The meat of any living animal was never 'meant' to be used for consumption by human beings. Even worse, we as a society have been "brainwashed" into believing that meat actually tastes good or delicious when in fact, it tastes horrible and abhorrent.

That hamburger that you're eating or that so-called 'delicious' chicken sandwich was once a living, breathing, healthy beautiful creation that was meant to live a long and happy life- not be a creature bred to be your 'quick lunch' because you as a human being can't think of any other alternatives to eat, or because there aren't many other options out there except meat.

People often believe that chicken isn't harmful or that chicken can be ruled out as a meat that is dangerous to the body, but this is nowhere near the truth. Studies have shown that all meat, including poultry, raises LDL cholesterol levels and are a key contributor to this. Research has also linked poultry to a higher risk of cancer too, with chicken containing PhIP, a well-known carcinogen that is linked to breast, prostate, and other forms of cancer.

The consumption of poultry meat has recently been linked to higher instances of gastroesophageal reflux disease, gastritis, diverticular disease, diabetes, and gall bladder disease. Many meat eaters according to research, were predominantly obese, overweight, or had a high risk of developing this.

Chicken and poultry meat is not healthy for human consumption and a human's body was not designed to digest meat properly. Nearly 65 billion chickens are murdered worldwide for food, and this is an unfair statistic to these extremely intelligent creatures who don't deserve to deal with this kind of fate in the name of human ignorance.

Poultry is also the reason to blame for most food borne cases of food poisoning, illnesses and outbreaks according to research. There is no benefit to consuming any form of poultry as food or protein and in turn it does more harm than good to a human's body.

Meat is responsible for heart disease and stroke in humans, yet true carnivorous animals never suffer from these ailments. Heart disease is the number one killer in the United States according to the American Heart Association. Eating any form of meat, even chicken and poultry contributes to this serious health issue.

Alternatives to meat

What can a vegetarian/vegan eat?

If you decide to not eat meat or become a vegetarian you will find you have hundreds and thousands of options and varieties of food out there and being a vegetarian doesn't mean your options are limited but more than usual, your options actually grow in number and strength believe it or not. Now this list does contain foods with cheeses, but it's extremely important to focus on being vegan and not vegetarian, and very important to eat vegan based foods with vegan cheese which are in fact very delicious and even taste better than dairy based cheeses.

Sushi without meat, tabouli, Fattoush, falafel, hummus, baba ghanoush, nuts, legumes, edamame, salads without meat, sandwiches with veggie patties, impossible burgers (which taste better than beef burgers in my opinion), lentils, vegetable curries (Indian food is packed with vitamins and nutrients and amazing spices and also has a large variety of tasty delicious dishes that are completely vegetarian or vegan) pizza (with vegan cheese or no cheese), veggie pizza, cheese, quesadillas, veggie fajitas, fruits, vegetables, French fries, tater tots, eggs, vegan yogurt, peanut butter, nutella, pasta with marinara sauce or veggies, eggplant parmesan, pasta primavera, bread, moussaka, chick peas. There are many Indian food dishes you can eat from chickpeas to potato dishes all of which are very delicious and hearty. There are meat alternatives such as tofu, soya protein, tempeh, seitan, spelt, oat flakes, black beans, chickpeas, and pea protein. Literally, most of what you do eat usually DOESN'T consist of meat contrary to what you think or feel. You might eat foods that have meat on them, but meat isn't as prevalent as you think or feel it is.

Now what you do you usually eat on a regular basis? Do you eat sandwiches for lunch, or maybe a chicken sandwich sometimes. You can't eat steak for dinner all the time, so what do you usually end up eating throughout the day? If you really think about what you eat and put things into perspective, you'll come to the conclusion that most of what you do eat doesn't always consist of meat or has to, and there are vegetarian alternatives for almost anything out there today. Also, eating vegetarian is simply healthier, and meat is completely unnecessary for a human to consume and generally has more negative and harmful effects than it does positive effects. Meat is linked to a higher and increased rate in mortality and is the number one reason for heart disease. Eating meat isn't good for a human being and eating a plant-based diet rich with fiber and antioxidants can help with healing a human being's body, immune system, and is the healthy way a human can eat and live their life all while saving the planet and innocent animals as well.

Meat needs to be banned

Meat needs to be banned from society and the meat and dairy industries need to be effectively shut down, and not allow the contamination and pollution of the planet and the disintegration and destruction of billions of animals worldwide and yearly. Better alternatives need to be served such as almond milk and meat substitutes. You can find comparable meat substitutes such as the impossible brand, Tofutti, chick-un, and varying other vegan or vegetarian substitutes for what humans consume as meat products.

Humans may crave meat in some form, but that is only because they have become prone to eating meat, their minds have become used to this and they have become brainwashed into believing that meat is a part of the human food group out there, or that meat is a necessity and essential for human growth and proper nutritional sustenance. None of these things are true. Meat is a toxic byproduct, and the meat people eat belonged to an innocent animal and their family, and was once a healthy living beautiful precious being that didn't deserve the fate they had. Meat is so toxic to human health that the WHO labeled it as a carcinogen similar to cigarettes.

The dangers of the dairy industry

Almond milk tastes better than conventional dangerously cruelly made cows milk, is nutritionally more solid for humans and digests easier in the human body. Humans don't have a digestive or nutritional need for other animal's milk.

Milk simply isn't a necessity for human consumption and on the contrary the consumption of milk leads to make human health issues and diseases.

Milk was meant for baby cows and calves and is meant to nourish and strengthen and young of cows, not for growing adult humans to steal and even do damage to their own body by consuming milk.

Humans have the capability to cook and prepare foods and to plan and use their biology and ability to think and cook, to create hundreds and thousands of different kinds of foods. It is not a necessity to consume meat in any form for we have a plethora of other options out there to consume, our bodies are not meant to ingest and digest meat perfectly, and animal meat can contribute to a host of health issues along with the unfair slaughter of billions of innocent animals worldwide yearly. We can use our biology, minds and technology to create and prepare a host of non-meat products and foods that are far more nutritious than meat is, for studies have proven that meat is nothing but hazardous to the human body. It is not necessary to consume meat not only for pleasurable eating but to sustain any form of nutrition that is viable to the human body. Plants, fruits and other foods provide the necessary nutrition that a human needs in order to thrive and function properly, and meat contains no fiber and no real nutrients that a human can't get elsewhere.

These beautiful creatures all have unique lives and personalities, and they yearn to live a happy, beautiful life full of joy and goodness just like any other creature does. When they are subjected to the harsh and brutal conditions they might be, it is worse than torture and something that should not be happening for these innocent creatures.

Chapter 7

Pigs Are Your Friend, Not Food

Pigs are intelligent, inquisitive social creatures who are very misunderstood and misrepresented. In a world where several holy religions deem the pig unclean and unworthy and too filthy to consume (which is a good thing), they are often the target of maltreatment and confusion by people who feel they aren't worthy or decent creations. Pigs are beautiful, highly intelligent mammals who establish social groups, sing to their young, and are extremely friendly and complex animals.

Pigs have a rich history of co-existence with humans. Pigs and people have very similar digestive systems and diets as well. Humans are pigs are both omnivores who eat meat, roots, and seeds. Food first brought them together. In Turkey about 10,000 years ago, humans settled into villages in Turkey and began living alongside domesticated pigs who invaded to scavenge rotten grain and fruits. Pigs and humans lived alongside each other in harmony in some form during these times.

By 1,000 BC, however, pigs were deemed unclean in the Book of Leviticus, and pigs weren't perceived as partners or friends any longer. The Israelites could eat any beast that "parteth the hoof, and is clovenfooted, and cheweth the cud." Pigs were not allowed to be eaten at the time afterwards. The Quran also gave out commandments that the pig or flesh of swine was forbidden for consumption. For this reason, a quarter of the world's population- Jews and Muslims, must avoid pork.

Now there is a misconception in this way of thinking and interpreting these holy books and scriptures and understanding. These books are not stating that pigs are evil terrible animals we must stay away from completely- they are merely stating that the consumption of pig's meat is harmful to humans, unhealthy and for these reasons is completely forbidden. In essence, pigs are being protected from consumption and from the torment that comes with human destruction and consumption of these innocent animals.

Pig meat is dangerous because it is considered unclean due to the fact that humans can contract trichinosis from eating pork, and because pigs are not strictly herbivores like cows and other animals. Pigs eat filth such as carrion, corpses, and feces therefore their meat is harmful to consume for human beings. Carnivorous animals such as lions, gator, pigs, and any animal in this category are forbidden for consumption within these specific religious beliefs.

Jews and Muslims were not the only ones who felt this way about the consumption of pork. In the great civilizations of Mesopotamia and Egypt, priests and rulers avoided pork completely, while the heathenistic often known uneducated romans loved eating pork, and created a pork-based cuisine for their era and culture.

Pigs today eat a wholesome diet of corn and soybeans, but people have new reasons to avoid pork.

The pig is a beautiful wonderful social creature. It seeks to live a happy healthy life just like every other creation out there. It too breeds like other animals, has children, friends, relatives, a healthy and active social life and enjoys being happy, healthy and interacting with its natural friends just like any other living creation does and exactly the way humans do. Pigs or any healthy living creation, especially mammalian in nature were not bred solely so they could be produced and created for food only and to be treated worse than an inanimate object or commodity, simply to be used, abused, tortured, destroyed and inhumanely murdered just so someone can eat a slice of pork with their eggs.

People are often fed lies about pigs being told that their living areas are filthy, and that pigs are in fact filthy animals when this is far from the truth. Pigs simply don't possess sweat glands and aren't able to sweat so they roll around in the mud in order to stay cool. They are clean animals and keep their toilet areas away from their living or other locations.

Pigs are highly intelligent and easily trainable animals, learning various tricks even faster than dogs. At 2-3 weeks old, piglets have already learned their own names and usually respond to them. As a matter of fact, they are the fourth most intelligent animals in the world only to chimpanzees, dolphins, and elephants, and possess similar cognitive abilities. Their intellect is generally higher than a dog's, some primates and even young human children.

According to research, pigs can do better on playstations than some primates and have the mental capacity of a three-year-old. They also can solve multiple choice problems and can use mirrors to find hidden objects and understand the passage of time. Their ability to use mirrors is a sign that the pig is self-aware and this is a characteristic once thought that only humans, elephants and a few other species possessed.

Pigs grunt to communicate with each other. Their grunt is very dependent on their personality and they socialize in this way and are highly socially intelligent creatures.

Newborn piglets can respond to their mother's voices and socialize with their siblings and mothers, and mother pigs communicate with their babies by grunting and sing to them while nursing. Pigs have amazing memories and can often remember things for years and can recognize objects as well. They are very social and often form close bonds with other animals and with each other as well.

Pigs give out a shrill, high-pitched squealing noise of up to 115 decibels, which is 3 decibels higher than that of a supersonic Concorde.

Pigs are not dirty animals, they're actually known to be very clean animals, and are some of the cleanest animals to exist. Their reputations as filthy animals come from the fact that they need to cool off in mud. Pigs that live in cool environments stay very clean and healthy. They are known to bathe in water or mud. In factory farms, they are forced to live in their own feces and vomit and around the corpses of other pigs. The conditions in these factory farms are extremely filthy and dangerous for these innocent pigs to live in.

They have their own very intelligent language of squeals, grunts, screams and oinks and communicate effectively with one another. There are 20 distinct sounds in pigs' vocal communication that humans have studied and recognized. Male pigs in fact sing songs to court females, and mother pigs can recognize their piglets by different sounds.

Pigs are incredibly social animals and have a wide range of amazing personalities just like any other animal and cats and dogs. Pigs can form very close bonds with other animals. Pigs often extend their social circles to other species and can recognize humans and other animals.

Pigs play with things the same way dogs and other domestic pets do. They fight, wrestle, jump and get excited at the notion of various things happening around them.

Pigs are known to have great memories and even have episodic memories which is memory that's specific to someone's personal experiences throughout life. They understand the concept of time passing by and have the ability to even plan for the future in some form which is both astonishing and amazing.

Pigs are very empathetic animals and have the ability to feel the emotional state of those around them. They are not creatures who have no feeling or care for others, yet so are other animals just like them. They assume what other pigs know as well and have other capabilities aside from being empaths and caring, kind creatures. Pigs are extremely sensitive creatures that can pick up on different things.

In the wild, pigs eat everything from leaves, roots, and fruit to rodents and small reptiles. In the United States, farm-raised pigs eat commercially made diets of mostly corn. A pig's best sense is its snout, and the snout is used to smell tubers and other roots in the wild, and they have an amazing sense of smell. They are able to sense smells from five miles away which is incredible.

Pigs can run faster than most people and actually can run from 11-15 miles an hour.

These beautiful animals are incredibly special beloved creatures that were never put here on this earth to become sole food for selfish greedy humans who have nothing better to do than to use animals for profit and food and nothing else. They should never be bred simply because the industry doesn't care to enforce any laws, and there are no real laws protecting these innocent beautiful creations that deserve a peaceful happy good life, not a life trapped in a slaughterhouse where they are brutally destroyed and murdered as if they are nothing.

In these wicked, terrifying conditions known as factory farmhouses and slaughterhouses, innocent highly intelligent, caring, sensitive pigs just like other helpless beautiful animals are treated as nothing but non-living or non-breathing commodities, with zero feelings or care, and without a care for how they feel about the brutal horrifying conditions they are forced to endure throughout their lifetime.

These playful, loving creatures are deprived of the mental stimulation, natural or even clean environment and anything they might need to be happy, healthy, sociable animals. Pigs raised in these horrific conditions and places display behavioral abnormalities, suffer cognitive and any form of mental impairment, and many animals are usually driven mad from the terrifying situation they are placed in.

It's incredibly important that we as humans do whatever we can to ensure that these innocent animals along with every other animal that is used in these menacing factory farms and these places where there are no regulations or laws being enforced and no care or concern for the welfare of these animals, get the humane treatment that they so deserve and are allowed to live the good life they deserve at the very least.

We can't just sit back and claim we are aware of these animal's conditions and situation for that does not change the current situation at hand at all. We as law-abiding citizens need to take steps to make changes occur and to make sure that any laws that are in place are strictly enforced so as to ensure that all animals on factory farms get the rightful life they deserve to live and a humane death, and that the concept of consuming animal meat altogether should be banned. We should create legislations and ensure their enforcement to protect these animal's rights, and most importantly we need to go vegan and vegetarian and never touch or consume any form of animal meat to ensure that these horrifying places stop the abuses that go on in them regularly without a shred of care from anyone out there.

Chapter 8

Chickens And Cows Are Beautiful, Sociable Animals

Who would think of eating cows, chicken, turkeys, ducks. These are after all, extremely intelligent, sensitive beautiful caring good animals who deserve only kindness and great treatment.

I grew up on five acres of land, and at some point, we had a cute little farm going on with two cows, a horse and some goats. Cows are incredibly friendly, peaceful, loving, and caring creatures who make great pets. Every animal being used and treated as sole sources of food and meat for humans happen to be some of the most intelligent, peaceful, and caring creations, yet this is what you'll find of most animals, amongst domesticated pets as well. Most animals are decent, caring, and kind docile creatures.

Most domesticated animals out there are decent, kind, gentle loving good creatures who only deserve to be treated with kindness and respect. So why are these innocent creatures being bred by the billions and used as food for humans. Why can't humans perceive cows, chickens, or other farm animals the same way they perceive cats and dogs? These animals are not on this earth and were not created solely to be consumed as meat for confused, brainwashed humans who have no clue or care for the plight of these extremely beautiful precious souls.

Jennifer the chicken finds herself on a different kind of farm. This isn't your ordinary farm. Chickens have some leeway here and live their lives in some kind of peace, not trapped in a warehouse in cramped, dangerous, filthy conditions. She has adequate food, water, air and can go outside and enjoy nature with her friends. This isn't what you typically find out there in the world of agriculture, and in the farming and egg industry. What you find is something too horrifying to comprehend.

Many animals are highly misunderstood

Chickens and birds are highly misunderstood creatures who people simply just don't know the facts about. People have come to a high misunderstanding that animals either don't have feelings, don't feel pain, or aren't sociable, social creatures with their own lives who deserve a good life the same way humans feel other humans do.

The complete opposite is true- most animals, birds, and mammals are highly sensitive, have great feelings and often even have greater feelings than human beings. They just like humans and any living being are extremely sensitive to pain and feel pain just like any person does. There have been numerous faulty untrue studies done that make erroneous claims that animals feel less pain or aren't responsive to or don't feel pain at all. Yes! Of course, animals feel pain, and many are more sensitive to pain than human beings. Animals just like humans do have pain receptors just like us and feel pain immensely and in some cases their tolerance for pain is far less than a human's tolerance but is definitely equivalent to a human's tolerance for pain.

The Uniqueness Of Chickens

Chickens are extremely intelligent and fun animals that are as smart as mammals such as cats, dogs, and even some primates. They are intelligent and emotional animals with unique personalities. Their intelligence is often underestimated and overshadowed by other Avian groups, and studies show people have biases and misconceptions regarding this aspect of the chicken. Though recent studies have proven that the cognitive functions of birds are very similar to that of other mammals and humans as well. The avian forebrain is actually derived from the same neuroanatomical substrate as the mammalian forebrain. There are in fact 25 billion chickens on earth at one given time. Chicken can actually remember over 100 faces of people and their own species and have excellent memories. They can even solve puzzles and let humans know what to do regarding the puzzles. They have the same concept of remembering and recognizing faces and people the way dogs and cats do.

A chicken's body is 75% water, and as chickens get older, they lay bigger eggs. To bring in hens, roosters actually dance to attract hens something called 'tidbitting,' and is a very intriguing way of calling on a potential mate. Chickens also enjoy sunbathing, and are known for laying out in the sun, something not everyone is aware of. Chickens actually experience REM and just like us, they dream while they're sleeping.

Just like human mothers, chickens actually talk to their babies while they're in the eggs, and then talk to them once they are born and teach them just like any other animal. They have around 30 different calls and ways of speaking with each other just like any other animal but have a more distinct form of communication they use compared to cats and dogs.

Chickens purr just like cats do. When they feel safe and comfortable, they will purr in their owner's arms. These cute inquisitive animals often don't mind working for their food, something known as contrafeeding, and studies have shown that chickens will push a button in order to get their food, rather than just getting it without pushing one. Chickens are able to see more colors than humans and have retina cones that can detect and perceive violet and ultraviolet wavelengths. They are also able to focus close-up and far away at the same time in different parts of their visual field.

Chickens have shown a big interest in images and prefer color images to black and white images. Chickens have remarkable abilities aside from their brilliant color and image recognition ones. The beak is a remarkable part of the body of the chicken. The end of their beak is comprised of very sensitive receptors which allow them to discriminate between a variety of substances, objects and textures. The beak is present to grasp and manipulate food items, and even non-food objects in nesting and exploration and drinking. It can also be used as a defense weapon during aggressive encounters.

They are incredibly social and have great memories and can easily recognize which bird is a part of their own pecking order. Hens have the ability to distinguish between sound and can anticipate the future. Chickens are incredibly sensitive and intelligent animals and are not just 'birds' who have no capacity for the understanding of complex concepts or subjects. Studies have even shown that baby chicks have the capacity to grasp numbers and numerical data and information at five days of age and can perform arithmetic operations to five objects. Therefore, chickens do share a number of very sophistical cognitive capabilities with other animals and mammals.

Cows are unique, cute animals

Cows are beautiful, special and cute unique animals and creatures. They are very loving and kind and enjoy being pet and being treated nicely, and in turn are very nice and sweet to those around them. Cows are gentle and affectionate animals and love receiving different forms of affection.

Cows are large, four-footed mammals with cloven hooves. They can have horns, which are unbranched and don't shed annually. Cows come in a variety of different colors, including black, white, red/brown, and can be spotted too.

The size of cows varies by breed, with the Chianina being the tallest and heaviest.

Cows are animals known to be ruminants, which means they have a complex digestive system that allows them to eat vegetation that may be difficult to digest. Cows regurgitate and re-chew their food, something known as cud-chewing.

Cows don't need much sleep and only sleep around 30 minutes a day. Cows are extremely social animals. They live in small herds of 20-30 animals and form close friendships with others in their special herd. They tend to lick each other which helps them bond better and has a very relaxing effect.

Cows are considered beautiful for many reasons, including their gentle fun nature, social behavior, and actually carry an importance to humans and the environment around them. Cows are very social animals and form strong friendships with each other. They help each other, groom each other, and become stressed when separated from their herd. They are known to be very gentle giants who are docile and curious.

They are a symbol of fertility and abundance in many religions and cultures. In Hinduism, cows are considered sacred and represent the Mother Goddess who is bountifulness and fertility.

Cows are a symbol of abundance and fertility in many cultures and religions. In Hinduism, cows are considered sacred and are believed to represent the Mother Goddess, who represents fertility and bountifulness. Cows are also celebrated around the world in different festivals or parades.

Cows are extremely affectionate and forgiving and love to be petted and have their bellies rubbed and stroked. They are extremely friendly and welcoming creatures who love to have positive interactions with humans and enjoy living a life of happiness and peace just like any other creature or animal out there.

Chickens and cows are loving, caring, kind, beautiful, sweet animals who are very social animals and who love the company of each other and that of humans as well. They are full of happiness and joy and possess unique characteristics that display their beauty and wonder. They are sentient, decent, good creatures who deserve a life of happiness and good just like humans do and are not on this planet to be bred in mass quantities or used as food for humans. They have strong feelings and form close friendships and bonds with others and possess deep feelings too.

Chapter 9

Treatment Of Animals Used For Food

More chickens are killed for food than any other land animal. According to Our World In Data, 202 million chickens will be slaughtered in a single day- that's 140,000 a minute which is really unfair and horrific. 12 million ducks, 3.8 million pigs, 1.7 million sheep, 1.6 million turkeys, 1.4 million goats and 900,000 cows are brutally murdered and slaughtered in a single day. Two trillion wild fishes are caught every year with 124 billion farmed fishes being killed annually.

Recent studies found something even worse to imagine- that meat from around 18 billion animals goes uneaten each year, with the majority being chickens. Animal slaughter has risen in the past fifty years- with 8.6 billion land animals being slaughtered in 1961 to 88 billion being murdered for food in today's day and age.

The numbers are staggering and extremely unfair to these innocent animals who have never hurt anyone and who have had to be born and bred into the most destructive, wicked system to exist when it comes to the treatment of these innocent creations. And yet, there are still no laws or regulations that can govern or guide not only the miscreants who are mass breeding and murdering these animals, but the gluttons who consume these creatures who are murderers as well for being those who purchase and consume these animals, which in turn creates a necessity for animal products and what keeps these dangerous destructive conglomerates going.

If there were only laws and practices that could effectively be put into place that would definitely be enforced- then something could be changed when it comes to these horrific practices that do occur in this society and world with regards to the extremely unjust and unfair breeding and consumption of these innocents who have no voices to stop this torture and murder that goes on in their brutal terrifying reality.

Animals everywhere who get abused and mistreated have to undergo horrifying conditions and less than par treatment along with torture and so many other atrocities that one cannot imagine. It is all very similar when it comes to abuse, torture, neglect, and a harrowing life full of nothing except fear, pain, torment, and horror. The treatment of animals used for food is a harrowing plight which needs to end somewhere. Animals on a planet full of such civilized humans with such great technology should never be bred or used for food or for any purpose such as clothing, accessories or for any reason to exist by humans.

Animals are not treated as the unique, individual, living, and sentient beings that they are. They are treated lower than any inanimate object has ever been treated and they undergo nothing except extreme torture, pain, mutilation, bludgeoning, abuses, and even boiling and scalding. It's shocking how the most intelligent living, breathing creations can get treated in such a horrifying, disgusting and disturbing manner. You would think that such a civilized society could have come up with the most humane methods of handling and dealing with real living creations but nothing of the sort has happened in today's times.

Animals, as stated before, have great feelings, sensitivities and even more so than human beings do. They are not creations that have no complex feelings or who don't feel at all and can easily 'deal with' or handle scenarios or situations. They are not ignorant, confused creatures who have no idea what is going on. Animals not only know they are being abused and mistreated, they know something just isn't right in their situation even if it's something that has gone on their entire lives. They do not 'get used to their situation' or 'succumb to it' or have no feelings for being kept in small stalls, cages and crates. They are concerned, terrified and totally helpless and have no power or say so and cannot do a thing to change their situation or the scenario they are in at all.

Animals have conscious feelings, and they know when they are not in a decent situation. They have feelings and want to socialize and be with their family or friends, and definitely do not want to be confined in a cramped horrific warehouse which is where factory farmed animals are usually confined to their entire lives. Animals have cognition, awareness, consciousness, and emotions.

Animals used and bred for food by the industrial meat industry and in factory farming and used and treated as nothing except inanimate objects and are treated as if they are of no importance and have zero feelings and those monsters participating in this horror have no care for these sentient, feeling creatures and in fact treat them lower than they would ever treat any inanimate object. Cows are shot in the head or have their throats slit in the most inhumane manner possible, pigs are kept in cramped filthy conditions, chickens are kept in the most horrifying cramped conditions without being able to move or turn around, and sheep have their wool stolen from them in the most brutal and barbaric way possible without a care as to how they feel.

Farm animals have to undergo routine mutilations and extremely painful, torturous procedures as part of standard routine, yet they are never given painkillers despite how painful these so-called 'common' procedures are. Hen's beaks are trimmed, turkey's toes are trimmed. Piglets have their tails docked, their baby teeth cut, their ears notched and males are castrated all without painkillers. Cows are routinely dehorned and branded as well with no ease for their suffering.

Even once the animal's injury is healed, they are never given painkillers, and it has been shown that these innocent animals experience chronic and severe pain wherever the amputation took place. While animals are on a farm, there's no process by which painkillers are given and on a federal level, there's no protection and nothing requiring the use of medication to be given to them.

Any pain relief given to any animal on a farm must be approved by the FDA and every medication must be used only for what it's approved for. Therefore, random animals experiencing extreme amounts of pain are not allowed to be given medications that have been created or were designed for other specific animals. It is a very unfair situation in an unfair reality which is the world of factory farming and the industrial meat and farming industries.

Veterinarians are held liable for medications not being used properly, so vets do not get involved in the affairs of these animals, though most are in dire need of proper medical treatment. It's important that these procedures are eliminated altogether in the farming and meat industry, or that something is going to be done with regards to the pain levels that are forced upon these animals who have no power to stop this.

Animals used for food are not considered to be living, breathing, feeling creations. They are perceived by the industrial and agricultural industry and all the cruel, careless workers who lack any form of empathy or humanity within them as commodities and all the brutalities they face are considered to be 'processing,' which refers to the tortures they end up going through in order for them to be turned into meat that ends up in the grocery store or anywhere around the world.

There are no effective laws protecting animals from a gruesome fate that the agriculture industry imposes upon them and worse the few laws that are there are never followed or practiced. These animals are helpless and born and bred into an industry that uses them for food only. Surely, you would think there are some rules set in place by the government to protect their welfare or interest in some form? However, sadly, there no rules or laws to save or help animals and the government has recently passed acts that slaughterhouses and factory farms can do what they want and hold their own standards and laws which in reality is just extreme and brutal torture, pain, suffering and painful violent slaughter.

Chapter 10

THE HORRORS OF FACTORY FARMING

There was a time when animals existed on small local owned farms. The animals were able to roam freely and enjoy their lives to some extent. This has been done away with since the discovery and creation of factory farming. Factory farming is the way that the United States and many other countries produce popular products such as burgers, cheese, eggs and milk, but the process only involves animal torture and unnecessary pointless cruelty. None of the injustices present in factory farms need to occur for there are far more humane methods of being able to produce animal meats, and animal meat itself shouldn't be allowed to be produced in any nation or anywhere on the planet due to the methods used upon these animals, and because they are important living creations whose lives matter.

The United States Humane Methods Slaughter Act is supposed to protect animals from 'needless suffering', but it does the complete opposite. There are no laws there to protect animals in factory farms or farm animals from the needless suffering and torture that is inflicted upon them in so many different formats while their short lives exist within the animal food industry. Factory farms were created based on the assumption that the 'factory' concept could be applied to animal farming.

Factory farming is a horror that no living or intelligent being deserves even for a second, and it is a disturbing sad fate that billions of innocent animals such as chickens, ducks, cows, pigs, turkeys, and goats must endure and live through in order to appease the palates of greedy confused humans who could care less about their lives. Factory farming causes significant damage to billions of animals worldwide, the environment, and to human communities as well.

About 99 percent of farmed animals exist on these harrowing horror conditions known as 'factory farms,' which are industrial-sized operations that raise large numbers of animals to maximize profit and minimize resources. These animals are kept in intensive severe confinement where their movements are prohibited in a major way, where they have no real resources or decent food, no good shelter, are in cramped confined horrific conditions, are deprived of any natural environments, and must live a life of torture and suffering and nothing else. This often leads to aggressive behavior towards other animals such as pecking, biting, and scratching.

As of 2020, there are 1.6 billion animals confined within the 25,000 factory farms spread across the United States. The number of animals confined within these factory farms has increased since 2002. Ninety-nine percent of animals in the United States are raised on factory farms. A single broiler chicken factory farm can produce about 500,000 birds every year. Factory farms do not care about the welfare of any living animal, only about the profits these animals can generate. Everything is performed without the animal's feelings or welfare in mind and there is nothing except cruelty done in these industrial torture chambers and warehouses.

On factory farms, animals are treated as nothing except inanimate commodities. Their feelings, rights, wants, need and desires are completely ignored and thwarted and they are used to fatten and grow, for resources such as milk, eggs, and meat and slaughtered when they are of no use for profits, or when they are large enough to produce the desired product. It is the most inhumane and disturbing system a person can imagine and there is no need in a civilized and ethical society to have such a callous and careless system designed to torture and destroy innocent animal's bodies and souls in order to milk the necessary goods out of these creatures.

All animals on factory farms live a life of pain, torture, suffering and extreme agony. Their lives are given no importance, and they are treated worse than even inanimate objects are treated. They will never get to see the light of day, enjoy the sunlight, bask in the sun as they were meant to do. The pig will never get to sunbathe as it does normally, and the cow will never get to graze upon the wonderful grass that nature meant for it to be a part of. Most will never breathe fresh air, and most are slaughtered without ever feeling grass beneath their feet. They are given no leeway when it comes to hazardous practices that occur and extreme torture is a part of standard farming practice when it comes to these loving, kind, inquisitive, caring creatures.

Inhumane treatment that is worse than horrors movies can be found on factory farms. Despite there being very few laws to somewhat protect animals, none of these laws will ever be implemented and that is a huge problem in this society. These animals are helpless and voiceless creatures and laws need to be implemented in order to save these animals from the rigorous cruelty and torment that goes on in these cruel concentration camps for animals. There are also truly no real laws that have been put in place to protect these innocent animals. It is a horrifying free for all on the animals at the farms and the gruesome evil practices that are done to them are known as standard farming practices and are even endorsed by many organizations.

Animals desire a good life too. They want to wake up to a great reality and future, peace and joy. They get excited and have a passion for living life more often than humans do. Animals become extremely happy and feel grateful and blessed when they are in a good situation and know it. They know when they are in a good home as well and are well taken care of and possess nothing except happiness and are in the knowing that they are safe and comfortable.

Animals living on factory farms or within the farming industry never live a life of happiness. Their short brutal lives consist of nothing except extreme pain, torture, and suffering that is unfathomable. From internal and external wounds to their intestines hanging from their body. This is a life of not even extreme pain but something far worse. They never get to enjoy nature or live in a natural environment that they were meant to be in. They are stuck indoors in a cramped filthy warehouse with noxious, toxic odors and mates of theirs alongside them with injuries and deaths that occur on a rampant basis. The procedures and methods that factory farms used need to be done away with and there needs to be severe legislature and laws that implement harsh and rigorous standards that these concentration camps need to abide by.

Inhumane treatment

Factory farms are riddled with not only inhumane treatment, but something too awful to describe. Cows are stripped away from their mothers upon birth or as very young infants only to steal their mother's milk so humans who do not need it can be the ones purchasing and consuming it and making the dairy industry richer than it already is. Innocent baby calves, especially males are deemed worthless and are inhumanely and gruesomely murdered after stealing them from their mothers, just so humans can steal and consume cow's milk.

Sows, female pigs giving birth are confined to tiny areas where they can barely move, while their innocent babies are basically mutilated and slowly destroyed and murdered by not receiving adequate space to exist and nutrition. Runts and piglets who are sick are often 'thumped' or banged against a floor until they are dead or almost dead, by the cruelest factory farm workers.

Chickens are not only debeaked but kept in the filthiest most cramped disgusting conditions with thousands of other chickens, and the situation is so horrifying that many chickens end up becoming cannibalistic in nature or cannot survive the rate of unnatural growth that occurs. Many chickens outgrow their bodies and are unable to move or walk and succumb to horrible diseases while being kept in these places.

There is nothing except inhumane, gruesome, and brutal treatment that goes on in factory farms. These places can barely be called farms, for they are nothing except the most merciless concentration camps which innocent, helpless, voiceless animals are subjected to without any power on their part or concern or care for their welfare by those carrying out these wicked and brutal actions.

Animals put through pain without anesthetics

Males are often castrated without anesthetics. Most or all animals are never allowed to experience the outdoors except for being on a truck on the way to the slaughterhouse, which isn't even inhumanity, it should never exist. These are only part of the injustices that occur on a factory farm. Piglet's tails are docked brutally without giving any form of anesthesia.

Cows must endure a painful procedure known as dehorning without any anesthesia.

The industry does this to stop horn growth at a young age. In very young animals, when horns have not fully formed, disbudding is performed by removing horn producing tissue either by hot iron or chemical means.

Cattle and goats are disbudded or dehorned to reduce the incidence of bruising or injuries caused by horns during transport and to reduce the risk of injuries to other animals and people.

Animals on factory farms such as pigs, cows and sheep have their tails removed, along with piglets. This is known as tail-docking.

These painful, terrifying procedures are done without anesthetics, forcing animals to endure immense pain and suffering. Piglets are innocent babies who are held in the air while their tails are docked, usually while they are crying or screaming out in pain. There is no one there to hear their silent and horrifying unfair cries while they are undergoing such a painful experience. In pigs tail docking is carried out within the first week of life, along with castration, teeth clipping, and ear notching.

Rather than give chickens more freedom and space they need in order to live necessary somewhat healthy and decent lives, billions of chickens are debeaked in the most gruesome methods, in order to prevent chickens from pecking at each other, something that occurs due to the cramped conditions they are confined in. As many as 15 chickens per minute are debeaked, and top beaks are cut by a half or two-thirds, while the bottom beak is trimmed by a quarter of its length.

Wild chickens or those kept in natural farming conditions do not become cannibalistic or need their beaks trimmed to socialize with each other. Factory farming produces these terrifying behaviors within these chickens.

Castration

Shortly after birth, male piglets are forced to endure castration without any anesthetic. This involves holding a piglet upside down and slicing and ripping out his testicles as he screams in pain.

This procedure is common and 100% of male piglets are castrated with no anesthesia or painkillers.

Murder of pregnant cows

Dairy cows are usually kept pregnant in order to continuously produce milk. Their newborns are stolen from them and murdered very soon after. It is a taxing and destructive, dangerous pointless cycle done to produce milk and needs to be stopped and eliminated altogether.

Once a cow's milk production declines, she is deemed worthless and is sent off to slaughter, and usually while pregnant. Full term calves are often still in their mother's body while she is being slaughtered, and they are often murdered on slaughterhouse floors as a result. There is nothing except brutal torture and death that occurs to these beautiful, amazing creatures and is something that needs to be stopped immediately with strict enforcement and laws that are there to protect and save these animals from these sick and disturbing actions.

Animals are confined

Animals are confined in the most harrowing and destructive unfair ways possible. In factory farming all animals are subject to extreme confinement, while an animal's natural habitat is eliminated altogether. Animals in factory farms do not get the pleasure of being able to run around on grass, eat from their natural habitats or anything close to it.

Pregnant animals are confined to gestation crates, babies are confined to small areas where they are force fed anesthetics, and piglets are confined to small, cramped areas where they are given no adequate shelter, food, water or air and are often subjected to a number of unfair abuses while watching their innocent mother trapped in the most unfair of gestation creates.

Chickens in the industry are kept in battery cases which has the same space as the amount of a lined piece of paper. Female pigs used for breeding are forced to stay in gestation crates where they cannot move or turn around for the duration of their breeding.

Four or more egg-laying hens are packed into a battery cage- a horrible wire enclosure that is so small that they cannot spread their wings. The hens end up pecking at each other's feathers and bodies.

Growing pigs are confined to slatted bare, concrete floors. They often endure overcrowding and boredom and resort to biting and inflicting wounds upon their peers.

In the dairy industry, cows spend their entire lives confined to painful concrete. To boost production, cows are often injected with rBGH which is a growth hormone that increases a cow's developing of lameness and mastitis- a painful infection of the udder.

It is extremely unfair to confine any living being to a small, cramped area where they are even unable to properly excrete their urine or feces as is the case with these factory farmed animals. Pigs and cattle are often stuck having to live and exist trapped in their own fecal matter for the means of getting rid of feces is not efficient and what they do have are slatted floors.

Genetic manipulation

Genetic manipulation is a huge problem in factory farms. Factory-farmed animals can be bred to have certain traits. Broiler chickens are created to grow bigger breasts, since the consumer demand for breast meat is huge. This is unnatural for the chickens and causes a host of terrifying and debilitating medical conditions as the birds age. A large number of genetically identical animals allow viruses to spread much faster and potentially become more virulent.

Thumping

This is a routine occurrence in factory farms and is disturbing and should never be allowed. Piglets who are not growing fast enough or who are runts or suffering from a bad castration are killed by being slammed against a wall or hit against the ground. This is called thumping and results in extreme suffering and a horrifying and painful death.

Maceration

Each year millions of male chicks are born into the egg industry. These beautiful cute little birds are deemed worthless because they are unable to lay eggs or grow fast enough to be raised for meat. All male chicks in the disturbing factory farming industry are slaughtered shortly after hatching, by being dropped alive into a grinding machine, or being placed in trash bags and suffocated to death. It is an abhorrent practice that should never occur and yet it is still common practice in factory farms today. A few countries like France and Spain were in the process of attempting to ban this heinous practice, but it is commonplace in the United States today.

Depopulation

Depopulation is regular practice within industrial concentration camps known as factory farms. Depopulation" or "culling" is the mass killing of animals on a farm. Methods that are considered to be acceptable by the American Veterinary Association include extremely grotesque methods such as suffocating the animals with gas or foam, manually slamming baby animals against the ground, and turning off the ventilation system in barns and allowing the animals inside to die a gruesome extremely painful death of overheating.

This is commonplace if animals have a disease like swine or bird flu. Recently, thousands of animals have been killed by these methods due to breakdowns in the supply chain because of COVID-19. During the Coronavirus pandemic there were thousands of innocent animals slaughtered using these methods and roasted alive in barns. There are numerous videos online that describe and show the horrors that occurred to these creatures. These farmers tend to claim this has to do with profit over anything else. There are no laws to stop these barbaric practices, and many agencies find them to be acceptable. Something needs to be done about the evils that are done to these helpless animals in farms worldwide.

Environmental Pollution

Factory farms cause a huge issue with regards to polluting the air, land and water around facilities. Manure from animals poses a huge problem in the contribution to global pollution as does the presence of these animals. Meat production accounts for 57 percent of the greenhouse gas emissions of the entire food industry. A single hog produces around one and a half tons of manure every year, and all the hog farms in the US produce a total of 167 million pounds of waste. This is equal to the waste produced by half the humans in the nation. Hog waste is especially hazardous since it's not treated before being released into the environment, leading to extreme groundwater contamination.

If we shifted to a plant-based diet, by 2050 greenhouse gases and mortality rates caused by food production could be reduced by 70 and 10 percent. The World Health Organization claims that reducing livestock herds would also reduce the emissions of methane.

Cattle are known to produce methane by their normal digestive processes. Methane is also produced when animal manure is stored in large holding tanks. Methane is the second largest producer of global warming after carbon dioxide.

The Union of Concerned Scientists claims meat-eating as one of the biggest environmental hazards facing the Earth. Animal agriculture is responsible for more greenhouse gases than the world's transportation system combined.

Animals must be fed properly, given adequate amounts of water, and they take up many acres of land. Eighty-seven percent of all agricultural land in the United States is used to raise animals for food. They produce manure which gives off methane fumes, and the farm animals themselves produce methane by their very digestive systems, many of them. It takes 2,500 gallons of water to produce a pound of beef, and only 25 gallons of water to produce a pound of wheat. The world's cattle actually consume food equal to the amounts of 8.7 billion people which is staggering.

By relying on a plant-based diet and eliminating the concept of raising farm animals for food, we will eliminate around 70 percent of greenhouse gases, and eliminate the torture and harm done to farm animals by an unregulated industry that is criminal in nature towards these animals.

Meat production wastes enormous amounts of water. Raising animals for meat takes up half of all water in the United States. It's responsible for more water pollution than all other industrial sources combined, because of the huge amounts of animal fecal matter spilling into our waterways.

There are very disturbing statistics that are there when it comes to how animal farming relates to the destruction of the rain forests. Rain forests are torn down as a result of animal meat and statistics show that 55 square feet of rain forest is taken down for every single meal with rainforest beef. Every six seconds, an acre of rain forest is cut down just for cattle farming alone, which equates to 14,400 acres every day. Seven football fields of land are bulldozed worldwide every minute to create space for farm animals. More than 80 percent of the Amazon rain forest that's been cleared since 1970 is used for meat production.

Faulty and exceptionally cruel slaughter practices

Slaughterhouses are often full of blood soaked and filled floors and animal parts everywhere. Cows are often shot or stunned with a bolt to their head. Calves are stunned with a bolt to their heads. Chickens are placed on a conveyor belt where they are shackled cruelly and hung upside down and go through a lengthy painful process of electrocution/stunning, and then having their throats slit brutally, and are then placed in a scalding tank where there are many instances of chickens even still being alive while undergoing these processes. They aren't even treated as commodities, because commodities don't get boiled alive or scalded or have their throats slit. Gas chambers are used to suffocate piglets and pigs and there is not a single intelligent or decent method that is used upon these animals. There is not a single manner or method the agriculture industry uses that is humane in any shape or form towards these beautiful, sensitive, intelligent animals, and what they endure is something even too gruesome for a horror movie.

Cows often fall and can't get back up and are dragged with chains and pushed across concrete floors with forklifts. There are many inhumane, painful, and forceful methods used to move cows which result in severe painful injuries including bruised muscle, torn skin and damaged nerves. Cattle prods are electrified sticks used to make cattle move in a specific direction. They damage cows and are extremely painful.

Many kosher grade slaughterhouses use even more brutal and inhumane methods for slaughter and will often prod and cut an animal after its throat has been slit and it is still alive. These are the most evil, pointless, barbaric, and gruesome techniques that anyone can use against just kind, gentle creatures such as cows and these beautiful animals who are treated as nothing except commodities and tortured during their lives and deaths.

With all the technology we possess in today's society, rather than using it to create either humane methods for slaughter, breeding or housing animals, it has been forgotten and is used to create the most abhorrent death traps used to inefficiently slaughter billions of animals in the most inefficient, brutal and cruelest ways possible. Any manner or methods used for slaughter aren't only extremely painful for the animal, but are nothing except extreme torture and mutilation methods that just get worse and worse.

None of the technology or advancements we have come to in the 21st century are known to be painless or humane methods for slaughtering, housing, or breeding any animal involved in the factory farming torture fests and extreme concentration camps they are known for. We can easily harness technology and use it to create the most humane and painless ways to allow any innocent animal to survive and be put to their death, but more so, to eliminate the breeding and slaughtering of farm animals altogether and to create plant-based alternatives to animal meat because the concept of animal meat just doesn't make any rational sense given the brutality and torture that is incurred upon these animals and in such large numbers, and the idea that there is just no other option and that these bizarre, twisted practices are perceived as humane and are completely legal and that there is no protection for these farm animals and animals out there.

These are considered to be 'standard' farming practices and are the most abhorrent cruel and brutal methods of handling or dealing with any living being. Animals need our support and help for there is no one to help or protect these vulnerable beautiful creatures from these barbaric, gruesome, and disturbing practices. The

Animal Welfare Act was set in place to protect these animals from this brutal torture, but there are no laws set in place to enforce any protective acts for farm animals. Animals are left vulnerable to legal torture and there is no one there to stop their tormentors.

Farm animals are playful, curious, inquisitive, caring and exhibit a love for others and life that is similar to that of our companion animals. They too yearn to live a happy, joyous life exempt from pain that they deserve, but this isn't what they ever experience as creatures being bred for food in the agriculture and farming industries. It's important to live a cruelty free, meat and dairy free life at the very least in order to protect these animals from these heinous gruesome acts and to help end the concept of factory farming on the planet.

Humans by nature were never meant to eat various types of cooked meats. Humans might be classified as omnivores, but we do not possess the biological make up of an omnivore in nature. Humans possess the biological makeup of an herbivore or frugivore, and our digestive systems are meant to digest plant and other substances and materials not animal meat.

All animals deserve to be happy and live a life of enjoyment and enjoy their foods, existences and experiences just like any human does. Every animal possesses extreme intelligence and is not just a mindless creature that doesn't feel or experience pain or pleasure. They feel pleasure, contentment and enjoyment and deserve to life a painless, healthy and happy life. Factory farming doesn't deprive animals of joy or happiness- a life on a factory farm and in the animal food industry is nothing except extreme mutilation, torture and gruesome agonizing painful lives and an even more painful death.

Chapter 11

The Horrors Chickens and Fowl Face on Factory Farms

Animals of all natures from ducks, goats, turkeys, sheep and chickens endure the tortures and terrors that come from being an animal bred and raised for food in the agriculture and farming industry within the United States and worldwide. Chickens are incredibly beautiful and intelligent creatures of God and were not created to be used as food for humans who have thousands of other food options rather than the chicken. The concept of chicken meat is highly misunderstood. While chicken is being touted as healthy compared to red meat, it still is a dangerous culprit for human health, contains no fiber, and does more damage to a person's health than good.

Chickens are incredibly sensitive, social beings yet their life on factory farms are nothing except something out of hundreds of horror movies. There is nothing that happens on a factory farm that involves any form of humanity towards these animals. They are treated as inanimate commodities and brutal torture and murder are part of common practice on a factory farm and towards chickens and all animals involved.

The life of a broiler chicken

There are different types of chickens raised for meat and for laying eggs. Broiler chickens are what they call chickens they use for meat. Meat chickens are raised in a large shed or warehouse overly crowded and cramped with 20,000 other chickens who share the floor. The air in a factory farm setting is so thick with ammonia, chickens can barely keep their eyes open. Waste covers the floors they walk on leaving painful ammonia burns on their soft skin. Their legs buckle and break beneath the weight of their grossly large genetically enhanced muscles, and since they are unable to move, they often die of thirst.

Broiler chickens are bred to grow at a very fast rate. Their breasts grow large to meet 'market demand', while their skeletons and organs lag behind. Many suffer heart failure, trouble breathing, enlarged muscles, and chronic pain. In order to make sure they keep eating, corrupt farms stop chickens from sleeping by keeping the lights on all the time. Many chickens compete for space, and they can barely move or walk. The constant competing for space makes sleep even harder. Many chickens die and their bodies are still among the living as no one is there to do anything to make their lives any easier or less polluted.

Chickens are usually transported to the slaughterhouse at just six or seven weeks of age. Prior to this, they often succumb to various forms of disease. Many chickens buckle under their own weight and due to all the stress that goes on in a factory farm and the conditions of extreme pain and torture, many chickens end up turning into cannibals and will eat other dead or sick chickens. You don't find this behavior in the wild at all.

Chickens in factory farms suffer from high blood pressure, swollen abdomens, and cardiac arrest. Their organs such as their hearts, lungs and tissues are weakened by their poor health and the stressful painful environment they are in. A single factory farm can often house a many number of chickens and they are in extremely cramped uncomfortable horrifying environments. Many chickens also develop various forms of muscle disease.

Treatment of male chickens

Within their first few hours, male chicks are discarded and macerated- ground up alive while fully conscious, in a macerator which is extremely unfair to these innocent babies.

In the United States 300 million male chicks are killed every year, which is around 10 chicks per second and ground up. This is called 'culling' and occurs shortly after the chicks hatch. Male chicks are deemed worthless to the food and agriculture industry because they cannot lay eggs and are not the same breed used for meat production.

Globally, around 7 billion male chicks are killed annually. Other methods of chick culling include burning, electrocution, suffocation, cervical dislocation, and drowning. In the United States alone around 34,000 male chicks are killed every hour in the egg industry. Despite the apparent evil and cruelty involved, these methods of mass killing are all legal in the United States and nearly all major egg producers in the country kill male chicks or get their eggs from factories that do.

France, Germany, and Austria were the first countries that had committing to banning chick culling, and Italy passed a ban that should go into effect by 2026. Even farms that consider themselves 'humane' and 'free-range,' practice the sick cruelty of chick culling and have not done away with this practice.

Treatment of female chickens

The female chicks go onto endure miserable horrifying lives in cramped cages or overcrowded filthy sheds and are used as egg-producing machines. Chickens have proven to be extremely intelligent animals even as babies. At just five days old, chickens can perform arithmetic and faster than human babies. Chickens have REM sleep and dream just like humans, and they communicate with one another and with their babies in the eggs. Baby chicks even communicate with their mothers while in the eggs.

Most of these intelligent animals are hungry, thirsty and cold while being trapped in factory farms which are generally warehouses. They are genetically designed by humans to grow large and very fast so they can be killed and sold as fast as possible. They become nothing more than products just being used to breed, slaughter and sell so they can become someone's dinner.

Chickens are often cramped in extremely large warehouses and are housed with thousands of other chickens. There is ammonia that fills the air in the area they are, and it usually burns their eyes. Lights are kept on in these death houses and artificial barns so that animals can eat, grow, and become fattened up for slaughter rather than sleep. They walk and exist in their own feces and extreme amounts of ammonia and are unable to walk as a result and their skin gets burned from this. They are unable to walk, and they cannot support their own weight because their muscles become overgrown, and their bodies grow much faster than they are supposed to. Most chickens are killed at only 6-7 weeks old.

Chickens in factory farms which are essentially warehouses face a terrible fate. They suffer from a myriad of painful conditions and diseases which produce a vast number of terrifying symptoms. Sudden flip over syndrome is one disease they face on factory farms. Chickens are often very stressed and oversized for their body. This condition is similar to a heart attack and a chicken suffering from it will extend their neck, flap their wings suddenly and die within minutes. Pulmonary arterial hypertension syndrome is another problem chickens face. This is an issue of high blood pressure in the lungs. They also have a buildup of water in their abdomen leaving it incredibly painful and swollen.

Chickens also develop wooden breast disease because their bodies are designed to grow too large far too fast, and their breast muscles become tough and wood like. They are unable to walk and spend their time lying down and can't move much. Many chickens succumb to having to deal with severe ammonia burns. Ammonia develops as these chickens must move and exist on top of their own fecal matter and waste. These burns sting their eyes and pierce their skin and is very painful. Many of these chickens are unable to move. They also suffer from green muscle disease. They are bred to grow abnormally fast, and their bodies and muscles become too large to keep up with. The cells of the breast muscle often die from lack of supply to the muscle fibers. This creates areas of green decaying and dead flesh. These chickens' bodies are essentially just rotting and it's unfair to them to suffer this way and there is never any veterinary care in factory farms.

The slaughter of chickens

Chickens are excluded from the Humane Slaughter Act and there is no legislation that ensures the humane slaughter of chickens. The other animals who are supposedly protected by the act face a fate of a very abnormal painful slaughter as well as companies and farms do not adhere to any of these laws. The slaughter of chickens is extremely brutal and inhumane. There is no mercy given to chickens or any animal in a cramped, torturous factory farm warehouse setting or in the slaughterhouse itself. Chickens, like all other factory farmed animals face a painful and torturous end to their short, brutal, unnatural, and painful lives. Chickens face a stressful journey to a slaughterhouse where they are trapped in very cramped crates. They are then shackled upside down by their feet known as live-shackle slaughter. Many birds will flap their wings violently and endure broken bones and injuries during this time.

The chickens then move along an automatic process and are immersed in a pool of electrified water meant to stun and leave them unconscious, however, the electricity is not enough to always leave them unconscious, and many birds actually lift their heads and end up missing the water. After this, a sharp and painful blade slits their throats to let them bleed out. The chickens after this are then submerged in a tank of boiling water to loosen the feathers from them before a machine plucks them out completely. Investigations have revealed that many birds are not properly stunned before they are slaughtered and must endure the full pain of the entire process. According to the USDA, over 500,000 birds drown in scalding tanks every year in the United States. Everyday hundreds of thousands of birds die in the most violent, painful way possible.

Treatment of hens

How the egg industry works

Hens are very good mothers. They chirp to their eggs before hatching and show signs of distress and worry if their chicks are in trouble. Hens are more alert when their babies are in distress.

Chickens are great communicators, with research identifying over 30 distinct calls with many visual displays. Chickens are also clever enough to deceive one another and can identify over 100 faces of animals and humans. Chicks imprint on their mother within 2-3 days of hatching.

Hens live a disturbing, painful and terrible reality as they are often locked up in cages stuck with many other hens and are unable to move or walk freely. Every year, the US egg industry exploits more than 300 million hens for their eggs. Their existence consists of two years of extreme misery and suffering.

Newly hatched chicks will go through a sexing room process. Workers will quickly determine the gender of each chick. Females will be sent for beak trimming, vaccination and a rearing facility while the male chicks are disposed of. This is because male chicks don't lay eggs and are of no value to the industry. They have not been bred nor genetically altered to be ideal for meat consumption, so they are killed soon after hatching.

The male chicks are disposed of by being shredded alive in a macerator, gassed, ground alive, or sometimes thrown into plastic containers and suffocated. Sometimes the remains of these chicks are used to make low-grade animal feed and filler. The methods of disposal depend on the region and country.

Right after sexing, the female birds will have their beaks trimmed. De-beaking is extremely painful and is almost always done without anesthesia and using a hot blade. Within the breeding stock, male birds may also have their beaks trimmed and the last joint on the medial and back toes cut off. This painful procedure causes long-term pain and issues for these innocent animals. De-beaking is done due to the high stress environments these hens will be in and in order to avoid any form of injury to other hens or any kind of harm or cannibalism that usually occurs due to factory farmed environments where animals are mistreated and confined to small spaces and do not receive adequate shelter or are in decent living circumstances.

A baby chick's beak is known to have an extensive nerve supply and is a very complex, functional organ. This can lead to acute long-term pain. This in turn can lead to behavioral issues, reduced social activity, lethargy and changes to guarding behavior. It can also result in reduced feed and water intake and thus dehydration and illness due to a weakened immune system. Chicks undergo vaccination soon after due to the high number of avian diseases that can be present.

Egg-laying hens end up laying an upwards of 300 eggs per year and begin laying at around 19 weeks. Hens are generally confined with 8-10 other hens in a single small battery cage, where they are trapped in a small, cluttered environment far too small for the number of birds packed in there. Cages are typically stacked on top of one another in rows and housed in windowless sheds with no access to the outside. As a result, fecal matter and waste from the cages falls into other cages. It is a very filthy and painful environment for these hens. Cages are made from metal wire and are approximately 20 inches x 20 inches (50cm x 50cm) in size. They will have a trough for feeding, nipple drinkers and a sloped wire floor so the eggs can roll onto a conveyor.

In some areas in Europe, battery cages are in the process of being eliminated and are being replaced by enriched or colony cages. Five to ten hens are often crammed in a tiny wire battery cage where there is not enough space for them. Cage-free farms are also horrifying for hens for they are kept in cramped and dirty sheds with thousands of others and have little to no space to even move.

Because of these horrific living conditions, chickens usually get sick and die and sometimes workers even kill large groups of them because of an outbreak or one bird shows signs of disease. Many times, hens die, and the others are left to live amongst their rotting corpses.

After two years, the hens who have survived lay fewer eggs and are killed since they're not profitable any longer. Some hens are sent to slaughterhouses where workers shackle them, hang them upside down, cut their throats and then they are thrown into hot boiling water, many while still alive.

Most hens are killed on farms in a very brutal manner, because it is cheaper than sending them off to a slaughter house. This is how brutal and evil this industry is. All it cares about is profits and what is cheapest for the company and gives no care or heed to the condition of the innocent animal or how much pain it has to go through.

Hens are often stuffed into boxes and then gassed alive. The gassing doesn't always work and if they do survive, workers then beat them or slam them against a surface. Those who still survive this are sent away on a truck.

The egg industry is exceptionally brutal as is the entire food industry towards these innocent chickens. It is an unfair and faulty system that needs to be changed in many ways. No chicken or hen deserves the brutality they must face or endure, and each and every animal deserves a fair chance at a decent life and fair and humane treatment of some kind, rather than the brutality they must face in this unfair world known as the food and egg industry.

Nearly 300 million turkeys are slaughtered in the U.S. each year – with over 50 million killed just for Thanksgiving – typically at just 4-6 months of age. The final hours of their lives are full of unspeakable cruelty, with more than a million of them dying during crating and transport.

Nearly 1 million turkeys are unintentionally boiled alive every year in U.S. slaughterhouses, where fast-moving lines often fail to kill the birds before they are dropped into the scalding tank. All of this cruelty, despite turkeys being sensitive and intelligent animals who form strong family bonds and even enjoy the company of human companions.

Chapter 12

The Torture Cows Face on Factory Farms

Cows are treated in ways one cannot imagine

The fate for a cow in the farming and the industrial meat industry, is too horrifying to describe, as is for any animal that is bred and raised for food. Cows are gentle, loving, kind creatures who make wonderful pets/children for people and are not meant to be used for food at all or to be stolen for their meat. The bond between a cow and its mother is a very sacred bond, and cows are very protective of their young and love them immensely, and the pain they feel when their baby is stripped away from them is similar to any animal and just like any human would feel.

Cows are extremely social and gentle beautiful creatures. They deserve happiness and a life of peace and goodness, not to be bred, abused and tortured the way these animals are on these horrific factory farms.

Cows are beautiful friendly creatures

Cows have been domesticated by humans for thousands of years. In the wild, they live together in herds and are nomadic in nature. They spend their time wandering grasslands and plains and grazing on the plants and flowers they encounter.

Mothers often give birth to one calf per year and feed the baby cow for several months producing a gallon of milk a day. Mothers have an instant and sacred attachment to their babies and nurture them just like any other animal does.

Cows form instant strong bonds with their calves. Right after birth, the mother will lick her calf clean and encourages the baby to get up and nurse. Cows instantly form strong bonds with their calves.

Many people have no idea that baby cows especially males are deemed worthless to the dairy industry and are either slaughtered soon after birth, or within a week of being alive. They live gruesome short lives where they are barbarically abused and treated as nothing, and these precious cute souls are then murdered by a stun gun or bolt to their heads in the most brutal of manner which is regular practice on a farm or factory farm.

The evils of the dairy industry

The dairy industry is a corrupt and brutal industry that uses cows for their milk and inhumanely slaughters beautiful and cute calves who were just born after snatching them from their mother and ripping them apart from her. Calves are stripped away from their mothers in as little as thirty minutes after birth, while their mothers cry and bellow out for them, never to be seen again. This is stressful and very traumatic for the mother and baby, and mother cows have been found searching fields for their calves for miles around, and will make loud noises and call out for their baby for weeks after. Male calves are deemed worthless to the industry because of their inability to produce milk and end up living short brutal lives where they are often abused and tortured in various forms or just mistreated badly before being murdered mercilessly. Male calves are either disposed of or used in the veal industry.

The industry is extremely faulty for inseminating and impregnating cows in order to produce extreme amounts of milk that is stolen from these cows, while their innocent babies are ripped away from them brutally and then either sold for veal or murdered right away. It's a faulty and disgusting manner of producing milk. With all the technology that there is present, there should be humane methods of being able to produce milk, or either allowing the calves to remain with their mothers and really to eliminate the process of milk in the consumer industry altogether. Milk is not a necessity for human health and humans do not gain any substantial nutritious value from it. Any vitamin D or calcium milk does have can easily be supplemented.

It makes no logical or rational sense to murder and brutalize millions of cows every single day in order to steal milk from them and to murder innocent calves whose lives are just as important and precious and who deserve to live a good long life, not be tortured and murdered brutally after not being able to be with their mother.

Animals have a desire to live- they desire to live normal, happy, healthy lives and enjoy being alive just like any other creature. Humanity and humankind are in a dire calling to stop exploiting and using animals for their own twisted pointless gain, for meager profits, or for any given reason.

Nothing the agriculture or factory farming industry does makes any sense. It makes no rational sense to destroy millions of animals per week and billions per year in order to be able to produce enough animal meat for the demand of human consumption. The manner in which these animals are slaughtered, abused or destroyed is quite horrific.

Methods of slaughter used:

Slaughterhouses are horrible places, but many animals do not even make it to the slaughterhouse and end up dying on the way. Around 20 million animals die on the way to transport. They deal with issues such as hunger, thirst, bad weather, heatstroke, respiratory disease, or starvation. They are given no food or water during transport and have to endure this for very long periods at a time. They're often crammed so tightly that they can't move.

When the cows reach the slaughterhouse, they are too injured or sick to walk or move. These cows are known to the meat industry as 'downers'. Most cows are too scared to walk and are shocked with electric prods or dragged off the trucks. Animals who do not cooperate are forcibly removed or beaten.

Many slaughterhouses beat cows with pipes, and vocally encouraging one another to do so, while the cows were on their way to be slaughtered. Investigations by animal rights groups showed cows being dragged by ropes tied around their necks and twisting tails in order to get them to move. Slaughterhouse workers often use electric prods on cattle to herd them onto the killing floor.

The methods of slaughter used for cows are extremely brutal and something that shouldn't be allowed and should be regulated but isn't at all. In slaughterhouses, larger animals like cows are forced into knock boxes one-by-one, where they're shot by a bolt gun to knock them out. The cows can tell what's coming and try desperately to get away. These guns plunge a bolt through the skulls of the animals and are meant to render them unconscious while they're killed—but this often fails on the first try. There are also bolt guns that jam up and get stuck in cows' heads, and animals being shot repeatedly until they're eventually unconscious.

The lines move really quickly though, and workers are often not trained well in the matter, so for many cows, the technique just doesn't work, and they are often fully conscious while being butchered alive. It is a very sad situation for these innocent animals born and bred into this unjust system.

After the animals are bolted, a door opens, and they fall out onto the kill floor.

The workers tie up the cows' legs, slice open their throats with a sharp blade, hanging them up to bleed out until they die. The workers then skin the cows' faces before cutting off their heads.

Animals are supposed to be unconscious before they're sliced open, but many cows, and other animals as well, are regularly found to be conscious on the kill floor, and even have to be stunned again. Many animals are still alive for several minutes even after their throats have been cut. The industry only cares for its own profits and the more animals it kills, the more money it makes. The meat industry has a workforce that is made up of poverty-stricken workers, and they seem to have no care for these animals and can't do much about their own situation. It is a very faulty, twisted, and unjust system for these animals that needs to be changed and regulated.

Chapter 13

THE TRUTH ABOUT A PIG'S LIFE IN A FACTORY FARM

Ninety-seven percent of pigs in the United States today are raised in factory farms, where they will never be outside in beautiful nature where they were meant to be, bask in the sun, breathe fresh air, or do anything else that pigs are meant to love and enjoy as wonderful animals. They are usually trapped in horrifying warehouses with cramped filthy horrific conditions, and can barely move most of the time, run, or play. They are kept on a diet of drugs that cause them to grow faster and keep them alive somehow. The drugs cause them to be crippled under their own weight.

The Animal Welfare Act prevents mutilation, yet mutilation is done all the time in these horrifying factory farms. Animals should be kept in species appropriate conditions, and if these acts were enforced then mass animal husbandry would end in all forms. If we calculated the number of innocent animals that are killed and used for food every year, we could reach the moon and back forty times.

These innocent animals are basically only commodities of food and products and nothing else. Their treatment far exceeds something worse than that of even insects out there.

The most intelligent of farm animals, swine raised in the confined feeding operations that now dominate the industry endure extremely inhumane conditions. They stand on slatted concrete floors, and end up trampling their waste and having to stand in it. Most sows still spend nearly their entire lives confined to "gestation crates," metal cages so tiny the animals can't turn around. Sick piglets are killed by being grabbed by their hind legs and slammed against the floor, a practice known as "thumping."

Pigs are mistreated in many different ways in factory farms. On factory farms piglets are taken away from their mothers after just three to four weeks. They are then put into metal-barred and concrete-floored pens in giant warehouses where they will live, until they are separated to be raised for breeding or meat. More than one million pigs die annually just during transport to slaughter, and 10 percent of pigs are "downers," animals who are so ill or injured that they are unable to stand and walk on their own.

Male piglets are treated in harrowing sad ways. They are castrated without anesthesia or pain relief. Also, without anesthesia, notches are also taken out of piglets' ears for identification and their tails are severed to minimize tail biting, a behavior that occurs when pigs are kept in deprived factory farm environments.

The way factory farms operate is very faulty and the system needs to change. These animals need to be given enrichment that allows them to exhibit natural behaviors. Hens need the space to peck, scratch, perch and dust-bathe.

This is a very similar situation with tail docking in piglets, she says. Pigs are very intelligent curious animals that need to root and explore their environment. In a factory farm, pigs have hours of free time with nothing to do. There is sometimes infection and outbreak where a piglet starts biting and it spreads and becomes a problem. There need to be laws to better protect these animals from the abuse and issues they have to endure in these factory farms.

Although the cruelty of this castration is undeniable, some food corporations claim that castration is necessary to improve the smell and taste. All of this pain and suffering is inflicted on intelligent animals in order to make a product seem more appealing to consumers, who have no realization that these injustices and abuses are happening to these intelligent, sensitive animals.

There are hundreds, sometimes thousands, of pigs crowded into factory farms. In order to identify each pig, workers cut off sensitive parts of their ears to create patterns known as "ear notching." The notches are cut into a pig's right ear to represent their litter number and cut into their left ear to represent the individual pig's number.

This is a disturbing and cruel practice that shows how companies perceive these animals- they see them as products in an assembly line and not as living, sentient creatures.

Mother pigs (sows) cruelly spend most of their painful lives in gestation crates, which are very small in width and length. They are far too small to allow the animals to even turn around and the mother sows are trapped in these crates most of their lives giving birth brutally, and having their babies abused, murdered or taken away from them. After giving birth to piglets, sows are moved to "farrowing" crates, which are wide enough for them to lie down and nurse their babies but not big enough for them to turn around or build nests for their young.

Pigs are genetically manipulated to grow so quickly that they reach "market weight" when they are only 6 months old. Due to their unnaturally large size and lack of space to move around, factory farmed pigs often develop arthritis and become unable to walk or stand on their own. They can become trapped in their own waste in dirty feedlots, fostering the spread of pathogens and rampant disease. Despite these risks, they are still loaded onto crowded trucks and transported to slaughter.

Pigs are usually shipped to slaughterhouses across the country on trips that take around 28 hours. They endure these long journeys—sometimes suffering in extreme weather conditions—without any water to drink or food to eat. Due to severe overcrowding, they also have no room to lie down and rest.

By the time they arrive at slaughterhouses, pigs are dehydrated and exhausted from the journey- assuming they survive it. Many will succumb to illness, injury, or even death along the way.

Piglets are separated from their mothers as young as ten days old. Once her piglets are gone, the sow is impregnated again, and the cycle continues for three or four years before she is slaughtered. This intensive confinement creates unimaginable amounts of stress and torture related behavior, such as chewing on cage bars.

Once they are taken from their mothers, piglets are put in pens, and they are fed until they reach the required weight limits and then are ready to be sold. Every year in the U.S., millions of male piglets are castrated (usually without being given any painkillers) because consumers supposedly complain of "boar taint" in meat that comes from intact animals.

Slaughter of pigs

An average slaughterhouse kills more than 1,000 baby pigs every hour. The pigs are stunned before their throats are slit open. They're left to bleed out, then dipped into scalding water to remove their hair. The speed of the slaughter lines makes it nearly impossible to ensure every pig is properly stunned before slaughter. This means many pigs are able to see, hear, and smell the pigs around them being killed, and they are then boiled alive when they reach the scalding tanks.

Innocent pigs endure horrific abuses and unendurable suffering and pain throughout their lives in the meat industry, from the day they're born to their brutal lives and to the day they're violently slaughtered. But it doesn't have to be this way. By making the switch to humane plant-based alternatives, you can stop contributing to this broken system that ravages thousands of pigs every day.

Health problems of pork

Pork is an incredibly dangerous meat to consume and is of no real benefit to human health. Pork induces a health hazard known as trichinosis and is damaging to the human health. It is one of the unhealthiest meats to eat and should be avoided completely.

Food poisoning in the United States afflicts 45 million people and kills over 2000. Pork products are carriers of pathogens such as listeria, salmonella, pork tapeworms, and E. coli. A study of pork samples taken from stores found that most of the samples were contaminated with staph bacteria.

Scientific studies have shown that consumption of bacon, sausage and hot dogs is associated with an increased risk of diabetes.

Pigs on factory farms are often fed antibiotics and sprayed with pesticides due to the risk of the spread of disease. These antibiotics are passed to people who eat them creating major health hazards for people. Consumption of these antibiotics through the eating of their meat creates strains of bacteria that are resistant to treatment.

Stop factory-farming abuses by supporting legislation that abolishes intensive-confinement systems. A company known as Smithfield Foods phased out the use of the crates in the US by the end of 2017 and plans to do the same for its international farms by 2022. Also, voters in Florida, Arizona, California, Colorado, Maine, Massachusetts, Michigan, Ohio and Rhode Island have banned the use of gestation crates. In Canada, the crates are projected to be phased out of use by 2024, although the industry is pushing to delay that conversion until 2029.

Stop giving your money to pig farms and slaughterhouses. Going vegan means eating to save innocent farm animals lives.

Animal rights are an important part of our life and world. Animals are important beautiful creatures who exist in our world and it's our place and job to treat them with utmost respect, love and care. Many times, people lack the desire to treat animals with respect and this is extremely wrong of them to do. Animals are just as important as you and I, and it's of utmost importance that we treat them with love, caring and kindness only.

Our world and planet is a great open space for every living being and creature and animals have just as many rights as humans should. Animals are beautiful, intelligent, caring wonderful creations of God who were placed on this planet for us to love and care for and it is our responsibility to care for them and give them unlimited love and respect, not consume them or treat them with disrespect. Being vegan and supporting the vegan movement is something we should strive to do and the consumption of animals and factory farming contribute to global warming, climate and serious pollution issues in our world. Factory farming is an awful system and injustice to innocent farm animals who have no choice in the matter. Farm animals are subjected to heinous brutalities and horrible treatment and have to endure extreme amounts of pain and suffering, and the system needs to change and new laws need to be implemented in order to protect these helpless creatures.

Chapter 14

Solutions To Factory Farming and Using Live Animals for Food

Solutions to Factory Farming

Animals enjoy being alive and they enjoy life just as much as humans do. They want to live and be alive and get happy at the "little things," just like any other living being does. They look forward to their days and their moments in life. Animals live their lives in peace and do not hurt or bother others and they do not deserve to be mistreated, abused, used or exploited in any way or form by this corrupt system that has now taken over traditional farming.

They don't have a lack of caring or concern or simply don't notice the fact that they're alive or in a situation of suffering or something bad, the way many ignorant people tend to perceive they do. Animals feel pain, sorrow, suffering just like any other creature does. It is very unfair to cows, pigs, chickens, goats, lambs, sheep, turkeys, and other factory farmed animals that their kind or nature is used as food for humans. Why do humans resort to destroying this many different animals anyway? There should be a limit, or rules and regulations set to protect these innocent animals that have been born and bred into this terrorizing, cruel and brutal food industry. Cats and dogs are not the only animals who feel pain, sorrow and a host of emotions.

There are no laws out there protecting animals in any form except animals who might be pets and factory farming is illegal and should be banned. Also, the concept of eating animal meat shouldn't be allowed in this nation or in the world and should be banned as well since humans and this society haven't come up with humane ways of handling or dealing with animals.

The animal welfare act provides no safety to farm animals such as cows, chickens, pigs, turkeys, minxes or foxes. This act only covers dogs, cats, guinea pigs, hamsters, rabbits and primates. Rather than protecting these animals from cruelty, the United States enables fur and factory farms to continue what are deemed

Solutions To Factory Farming and Using Live Animals for Food

"common farming practices. A common farming practice is an action that, if it is common across farms, is inherently considered legal. The exemption takes no stance on whether or not the action is humane or causes suffering to the animal. There are numerous ways in which farms utilize common farming practice laws to maximize efficiency in their operations without consideration of animals.

In recent decades, more people have become increasingly aware of the plight of factory farmed animals and other animals out there and have tried their best to advocate for these animals in various ways. There are many solutions out there to factory farming and using living animals for food. Humans are not in dire need to eat or consume meat and are not deficient or lacking in protein. They are able to eat a variety of other foods and can be nutritionally sustenant on these foods.

Meat substitutes can be created through different plant products and can easily be readily accessible for the general public to eat and to utilize.

Creating legislature to protect and give animals rights and create rules

New legislature needs to be created to give protection to animals in factory farmed settings and to animals in farms so that they're protected and given rights and allowed the right and place to live safe, comfortable, lives while they are in these circumstances, and humane deaths if factory farming is still in continuance or happening.

The Welfare and slaughter acts and laws provide no protection for animals and are not regulated or enforced at all. There needs to be strict legislature out there with rules and regulations put in place and enforced in order to create brand new laws that give these helpless innocent creatures voices and protection. Animals are helpless and voiceless creatures and rather than giving them any rights or protection, the opposite is done- they are in fact taken advantage of for being unable to protect themselves in these circumstances and are heavily abused, mistreated and given no proper or adequate shelter in factory farmed settings.

Lab Grown meats

Lab grown meats which are also called cultured or cultivated meat, is grown from the cells of an animal, without any need to slaughter an animal to obtain the meat. The animal's cells are cultivated in stainless steel drums called bioreactors, which are engineered to encourage replication of cells or growth of biological mass. The products that result from this process have been welcomed with enthusiasm, due to their potential to replace the millions of animals being raised on factory farms around the world. Because cultured meat is produced in laboratory environments, it does not suffer from contamination issues that are present in traditional meat producers, such as antibiotic resistance and foodborne and other illnesses.

Lab-grown meat is made of the same cells that make up meat from slaughtered animals. The cultured meat is produced in labs, while traditional meat requires the slaughter of animals.

The concept of lab grown meat starts with animal cells. If the cells are collected directly from an animal, the animals do not need to be slaughtered. Once the cells have been gathered, they are placed into cultivators where they are provided with a growth medium to encourage them to multiply. The use of a scaffolding structure trigger cells to turn into fat, sinew, and other elements that help to recreate the textures that occur in farm-raised meat.

Lab-grown meat does not require the use of antibiotics, so its production does not contribute to this health crisis. There are no animals involved once the cells have been collected, so it does not contribute to animal related diseases which are prevalent in factory farms and in animal agriculture which can be a source of pandemics and other health related crisis and issues.

Consuming plant-based meat substitutes

Chickun is a very popular meat substitute and even looks and tastes like real meat and can easily be substituted for chicken in any dish or in anything a human eats. There are many numerous meat substitutes out there from specific brand name companies that can be used in place of meat and that taste and feel just like meat.

Humans are not lacking protein, and on the contrary, we live in a society where protein is heavily over consumed leading to a host of health issues. There is no notion where the myth of protein deficiency comes from, but we as a society are not deficient in protein at all. On the contrary protein is very readily accessible, there is an abundance of it and most people actually consume protein in all types of unhealthy sources, such as dairy and meat. It is a general myth that humans are in dire need of protein sources.

We can use our abilities and technology to create a powerhouse of meat substitutes for the entire planet to eat. Many humans crave meat and that's because they have become brainwashed into believing that meat is good and tastes good and mentally and psychologically and physiologically have decided to choose to eat meat as opposed to the normal reaction of potential disdain for it. Humans have become psychologically ingrained into desiring meat in some form because their minds have become accustomed to consuming it.

Eliminating dairy products in our diet

Dairy is not a necessity for human consumption. The dairy industry is a dangerous faulty and corrupt system that eliminates the lives of millions of innocent cows yearly, even billions, and slaughters calves as if they are of no importance.

Humans do not need to consume dairy in their diets. Cow's milk is created solely for baby cows, not for human beings. Cow's milk in itself holds no nutritious value for a human being, though it is a misconception that it's rich in vitamins which it may be, but humans can easily use substitutes such as almond, soy, oat or other types of 'milk' products that are dairy-free.

Cow's milk is in fact hazardous to human health and does more damage than it does good. Humanity has just become brainwashed into believing they need to drink cow milk for any given reason, or to sustain nutritional needs for vitamin D, calcium and other nutrients. These nutrients can be found in a variety of products and in vitamins as well. Again, cows' milk is created solely for baby cows to drink and to sustain their nutritional needs. The dairy industry works in the manner that it keeps innocent mother cows constantly impregnated and viciously steals the lives of their babies right away using them for veal or murdering them very soon after, just to be able to utilize and steal the mother's milk. This is the most inhumane, twisted and unjust system one can imagine.

Solutions to the industrial meat industry

Stay away from all dairy

It's imperative to stay away from all dairy foods and dairy based foods due to the fact that the dairy industry is extremely corrupt and does so much evil to innocent cows and calves out there. This is a clear solution to the industry and to eliminating the issues present in the system out there. There are many nutritionally sustainable replacements out there readily available to the public and as viable substitutes for all forms of dairy foods from sour cream to cheese that people can consume as opposed to the unhealthy dairy that also can be hazardous to a human's health.

Eat plant-based foods

We must eat plant-based foods only, rather than any animal-based foods in order to stop and eliminate the cycle of pain and torment that is inflicted upon innocent animals out there in society. It is imperative that we eat only a plant-based diet incorporating vegetarian and vegan foods if possible and spread the word to those we know regarding this as well. Eating meat is not a necessity in order to sustain human nutritional needs and on the contrary is full of health hazards and contributes greatly to global warming and other climate issues on the planet. Eating plant foods contributes to a healthier body, better nutritional sustenance overall and a healthier climate and planet for everyone.

Cut down your intake of animal meat

Our intake of animal meat needs to be cut down upon or eliminated. It is of great importance that we live in a world where the consumption of animal meat is far less than it is now. People have become accustomed to eating large amounts of animal meat and find this normal or okay, when it is not. In order to not support or profit the industrial meat industry, we and those close to us, need to eliminate and cut down our consumption of any form of animal products or meat.

Eat free-range and grass-fed meat

If you are going to eat meat, make sure you purchase it from small farms that raise their animals in a humane and healthy environment and not from large corporations that fund factory farms. Free range and grass-fed meat is from animals that have been raised in the open air and allowed to roam freely and who have had the chance to engage in natural behaviors rather than being confined to small spaces. Free-range meat is generally considered to be healthier and more humane than meat from animals that are confined or fed a high-calorie diet. Free range or grass-fed meat is generally healthier and has higher nutrients as well. It is often higher in protein, omega-3 fatty acids, beta-carotene, and vitamin E than meat from animals that are confined or fed corn.

Join Advocacy Groups

Joining advocacy and animal rights groups is one very effective way and method of being able to combat and fight the higher ups that have put these faulty bills and this legislation into effect. Joining groups such as PETA and protesting can have a strong impact on helping others become more aware of the global issue of animal rights needs that is plaguing our society today. Volunteer at local shelters, donate to animal rights charities and eat locally. Do whatever you can to help assist with the continuing fight against the agriculture industry and to help animals around the world everywhere. Sign a petition or start one- your voice matters and together with others you can stop the evils that are happening to innocent animals and you can make a change yourself. Conserve energy as well to assist with the impact that eating meat has had on global climate change as well.

Meat needs to be banned

Meat needs to be banned from society and the meat and dairy industries need to be effectively shut down, and not allow the contamination and pollution of the planet and the disintegration and destruction of billions of animals worldwide and yearly. Better alternatives need to be served such as almond milk and meat substitutes. You can find comparable meat substitutes such as the impossible brand, Tofutti, chick-un, and varying other vegan or vegetarian substitutes for what humans consume as meat products.

Humans may crave meat in some form, but that is only because they have become prone to eating meat, their minds have become used to this and they have become brainwashed into believing that meat is a part of the human food group out there, or that meat is a necessity and essential for human growth and proper nutritional sustenance. None of these things are true. Meat is a toxic byproduct, and the meat people eat belonged to an innocent animal and their family, and was once a healthy living beautiful precious being that didn't deserve the fate they had. Meat is so toxic to human health that the WHO labeled it as a carcinogen similar to cigarettes.

Meat is not a necessity for protein or for human consumption

Meat is not a necessity. The truth is the human digestive system is not designed or equipped to digest and handle meats. Carnivores have specific kinds of digestive systems, and we have long intestines to be able to properly digest plant products and fibers. Most humans have overconsumed protein, and we are not in a state of protein deficiency. Humans biologically are in fact plant eaters and omnivorous because they can eat more than just plant foods but nuts, seeds, legumes and a wide variety of other foods as well.

In fact, animal meat is a huge hazard to the human body, and does irreparable damage to it causing heart disease, cancer and diabetes. This goes for the acclaimed white meat too which is known to raise cholesterol levels drastically. Animal meat is destroying the environment as well as murdering billions and yes that is billions of innocent beautiful helpless creatures worldwide.

Humans have become accustomed to eating meat and there are few other options out there. When you go out to restaurants meat is the primary food substance on most menus and the rest are considered "sides." Meat is considered to be the main course, and it is difficult to find anything other than meat as a main part of a meal. It's a very sad situation for if there were other alternatives such as vegan alternatives and meals then people wouldn't be brainwashed and resort to eating only meat at restaurants or in their daily lives. They feel meat must be a part of their food diet or what they should eat but this is further from the truth. Meat isn't something that should be part of a human's main diet, on the contrary, humans should be eating other substances that aren't meat such as legumes, fruits, or vegetables as part of their main food diet and there are a variety of foods that can be created using vegetables and alternative sources of protein.

Also, humans aren't deficient in any form of protein so it's confusing as to why they have become so ingrained into believing they are, and that protein is such an important and necessary ingredient for intake. Since humans aren't deficient in protein it should be the least of their worries when it comes to food substances that they're lacking in.

Our long intestines indicate we have an anatomy designed to digest plant products not meat and we do not have the acids that carnivores do that's why they can eat and digest raw meat. Raw meat would make us sick and kill us. Our stomach acid is not even close to that of a feline by any means. Our make-up is nowhere near anything close to that of a carnivore. Carnivores also don't get heart disease and the kinds of diseases most humans get because we get that from our faulty meat-based diets primarily.

Herbivores can eat not only plants or whatever type we can be classified as but nuts, seeds and legumes as well as rice, oats and other products. Humans are not carnivores or close to being meat eaters.

Humans are not hunters who are known to kill their prey. We do not possess the capability or biological means to tear or rip apart flesh and do not consume blood. All carnivores and most omnivores or all consume raw flesh in some form. Our teeth are also indicators that we are not meat eaters, and we have incisors that are designed to rip apart plant products not meat.

There is no necessity for human beings to consume animal meat by any means there are plenty of other options for human beings and we can easily live a vegan and vegetarian lifestyle on this planet and do away with me eating completely

Human beings do not have the desire deep within or biologically to consume meat, and we do not possess the digestive systems to be able to digest or handle any form of meat. Meat tends to putrefy in the body create disease and is known to be acidic in nature and harmful for the human body. Meat contains no fiber and no real nutritious needs or is of necessity or real sustenance to the human body.

Factory farms need to be eradicated, and new solutions put into place

Factory farms need to be eradicated altogether, and new alternatives need to be created right away in order to allow innocent animals the rights and life they deserve to have and live. No animal deserves to be born in a factory farm setting and live a life of the horror and torture these animals face on a daily basis and throughout their short terrifying and painful lives. With the concept of meat substitutes, alternatives and lab grown meats, the case for animal equality can be settled in order to allow animals to not be brought into the world of being products and commodities in the food industry. The mass breeding of animals in order to create and generate mass amounts of animal meat products needs to be done away with completely. Animals are not here on this planet to be used solely for food, and no creature deserves to be bred into the food industry to be abused and mistreated because they are perceived only as a product and as a commodity.

With a little bit of help and a lot of togetherness, we can find solutions to eradicate the system that has been designed to destroy and terrorize innocent animals, and create new and improved solutions to allow animals in factory farmed settings to live comfortable, decent lives, and to live in settings that allow them to exhibit their natural habitat and be able to breathe fresh air, roam natural land, eat natural foods and be able to live in a comfortable environment, rather than one in a factory generated farm.

Animals are just as important as you and I and yet there are many who believe that they don't deserve to have the same rights humans do. We as humans need to treat animals with the same importance and give them the same rights we give to ourselves. Animals possess feelings, thoughts, and have love within themselves just like we do. Animals have gifts and talents just as we do and are beautiful creations of God.

The consumption of meat has caused a lot of problems in the world and in society. It contributes to extreme amounts of global warming, climate issues, pollution and causes problems and is a health hazard for humans as well. The necessity for meat is more of a farce than what is really needed. We should focus on being advocates for animals, support the vegan movement, and rather than consuming animals saving them and creating laws and rights to protect these helpless innocent creatures.

We should strive to do what we can to save these animals as they are helpless innocent creations of God who deserve to be treated with extreme amounts of respect and love. Animals are the most beautiful creatures who deserve only unlimited amounts of respect and love, not to be exploited and mistreated by an evil corrupt industry that only cares for its own profits and doesn't give a care about their feelings, need or desires.

www.ingramcontent.com/pod-product-compliance
Lightning Source LLC
LaVergne TN
LVHW021822060526
838201LV00058B/3479